"A catalog of uplifting thoughts, lessons, and experiences."

JONATHAN CRUZ & CHRISTOPHER RODRIGUEZ

The cover is an esoteric artwork that shows the left and right brain. It represents the opposite polarities of the mind. Different hemispheres and duality of the brain. Left brain and right brain. Logical and emotional. Sun and earth. Electric and magnetic. Masculine and Feminine. Yin and Yang. Straight and rigid thinking vs. creative free flowing spontaneous ideas.

GET HOME SAFE

A catalog of uplifting thoughts, lessons and experiences

Copyright © 2023 by Jonathan Cruz & Christopher Rodriguez

All rights reserved. No part of this publication may be reproduced, distributed, or transmitted in any form or by any means, including photocopying, recording, or other electronic or mechanical methods, without the prior written permission of the publisher, except in the case of brief quotations embodied in critical reviews and certain other noncommercial uses permitted by copyright law.

DEDICATIONS

Small decisions can make all the difference in our lives. A single choice made in our youth has the power to shape the course of our entire existence. Growing up in the Bronx, within the confines of the inner-city housing projects, a positive influence was paramount to my success. The world around me dictated that I join gangs and seek honor through the senseless murder of individuals from my own community. Drug dealers promised a way out of our dire circumstances, offering one of the leading causes of stunted growth: drugs. The average person lacked the power to impact our lives, as they usually kept their distance or moved away as soon as possible. Mothers struggling to provide for their children had no guidance to help their boys transition into men. Statistics dictated that we would remain in the same predicament we were born into, with any progress being minimal at best. The music we listened to idolize this way of life, painting it as the only path to success. The millionaires we knew were not athletes, but those who glorified a life of crime and violence.

    I want to be the person that I needed when I was young. I want to serve as an example that it is possible to succeed while being true to oneself. You don't have to conform to societal norms or follow the path of violence and destruction. You can be uniquely yourself and still make a difference.

This book is my blueprint, my legacy. I hope that someday it will be given to young children growing up in the inner city, just like me. To those who know right from wrong but need tangible proof that consistency and perseverance can lead to a better life. This is for you, young Jonathan Cruz, and for all the other children who deserve a chance to rise above their circumstances and make their mark on the world.

-Jonathan Cruz

This is dedicated to the children of the future—those who are often neglected due to their parents' demanding work schedules and lack of quality time. These children are handed tablets, allowing someone else's agenda to shape their upbringing. They are subjected to an education system that molds them into employees rather than independent thinkers. Furthermore, the radio and music industry manipulate their young minds with murder-themed music, negatively influencing their behavior. The entertainment industry also contributes to their premature sexualization, diverting their focus from intellectual growth. These children possess a deep awareness that something is amiss in the world, and they retreat to the safety of their rooms, seeking answers to overcome the challenges imposed on them at birth. Yet, they harbor a burning desire to fight back and create a better future.

This book is for the fierce children of the future: the children who the public education system couldn't connect with, the ones who refuse to be molded by the corrupt industries of entertainment, music, education, military, medicine, technology, pharmaceuticals, agriculture, and fluoridated toothpaste. They won't be fooled by the millions of dollars these industries invest to manipulate their young minds for their own profit.

We know that old dogs can't learn new tricks, but we won't let the same be true for us. We are determined to think independently, to resist easy manipulation, and to fight back against the status quo. We will question everything, and evaluate the information they've given with a critical eye.

We understand that having high standards, living by principles, and incorporating day-to-day positive habits benefits not only ourselves but also our families, our communities, and humanity as a whole. These children won't be satisfied with blind acceptance of the world as it is. This book is dedicated to the future rebels, the ones who will defy the corrupt powers and shape a better world.-

-Christopher Rodriguez

THE PHONE CALL

By Jonathan Cruz ☀

For all eleven-year-olds, December means Christmas is approaching. It means unwrapping gifts and getting a week or so off from school. I was the oldest at the time of three boys in a single mother household. Conversations between my brothers and I were about what wrestling toys we were hoping for or games. December was usually full of joy as we anticipated the holidays.

It was a typical Saturday morning and me and my brothers started the morning off with a bowl of cereal and some Saturday morning cartoons. We had a one-bedroom apartment, but the living room was made the boy's room. A queen-size bed and a couch that we shared with a 32-inch fat-back tv. My brothers and I usually would start a fight with each other and then shortly after, we'd play together again some more.

Grandma recently bought us the new NBA 2k with Iverson on the cover, so my brother Chris and I would go to battle every day on the game. After losing a game with my brother, I decided to not play anymore and just laid in bed while my two younger brothers played something else. I began to overhear my mom talking on the phone in the kitchen with one of her friends. I usually didn't care to be nosy as the conversations didn't interest me much. Usual gossip about shows, other people, and just adult life. This conversation drew my interest at this age because my mom sounded hurt. My initial thoughts were, *This is about my stepfather leaving us.* I was the only son who wasn't his, so our relationship wasn't the greatest. I endured occasional whippings and verbal abuse, so him not being with us anymore was a sigh of relief. This conversation was not solely about him though. My mom told her friend, "I have no clue how I'm going to get these kids their Christmas gifts. I have nothing, I'm getting evicted, and these kids at least deserve a decent Christmas." This carried on for about a ten-minute back and forth which I also heard my mother decline the help offered from her friend.

At eleven years old, this brought awareness and sparked something. As the oldest son, and my stepfather not around, nor was my biological father ever around, I knew I had to accept a new responsibility this young. I didn't understand how it would get done or what I needed to do, but my love for my mother and hearing her cry for help allowed me to know this was something I needed to fix.

The joy we had on Christmas Day and seeing her so happy that her boys were joyful opening the gifts she did provide was beautiful. I knew she gathered whatever change she had to get us what we asked for, and I was grateful. I made sure to express that even more this time, knowing the situation.

This conversation didn't make me a man, as I was merely a boy. I wasn't even a teenage boy yet but this brought awareness. This sparked rage in me to utilize as fuel. I thought, *Why did my father never come around and help? Why did my stepfather give up on us? What can I do to help? Why were we living like this? What would happen if we became homeless?* This fuel would carry on with me until I was able to find answers—until I was able to provide and do something more for us. This is when I chose to be the person my family was waiting on. Why leave those expectations to the next person to save us when I can be him? As a child, they feed us the cliché saying of you can be anything you put your mind to. Why not me? I chose to break the generational curses. I chose to be the inspiration for generations to come of my last name. I chose to make sure I am the one to lift my family up when they fall. I chose to be him. This is the wisdom and experiences I've accumulated along my journey. This is that same boy 20 years later from that phone call….

THE SUN VERSUS THE CLOUD

By Christopher Rodriguez

In my teenage years, I knew I had to leave my hometown, Dunkirk, NY. My mother drilled it into my head when I was in high school: "You're either going to college or the military, but you aren't staying here." She feared I would fall into the small-town mindset of the 5 D's of Dunkirk: drama, drugs, dollars, drinking, and dick. People rarely focused on anything else. It's a self-centered, individually focused mindset to become addicted to things that don't uplift you, your family, your community, or humanity, preventing collective personal growth.

From a young age, I was very curious about the world. I questioned everything and rarely accepted what someone told me without experiencing it for myself. After high school, my life followed this trajectory for ten years: I went through Marine Corps boot camp, Marine Corps infantry training, and joined the Marine Corps fleet. Upon moving to California I started feeling homesick. Eventually as I explored I started making new friends in the Marine Corps and exploring California. My mind evolved at a fast pace as I embarked on new adventures. I began meeting different women which eventually led me to having a daughter. I continued undergoing more training, changing jobs and units, forming new friendships, going on deployments to new countries missing the first seven months of life of my daughter. My mind was further expanded experiencing new and diverse cultures and ideas. I acquired trustworthy leadership skills by being entrusted with the defense of a base in Jordan and other lives. We all returned safely to the U.S. After deployment I did have a hard time adjusting back to the normalcy of the states. I was emotionally unstable and acquired an addiction to promiscuity. I lacked leadership in my own relationship and in turn it became very toxic. Eventually leading me to leave the military I immediately began experimenting with marijuana again. It was therapeutic for a time. My partner and I started a successful business eventually obtaining a meeting with Kendrick Lamar but we were late to meeting and missed the opportunity. This led into a hard fought battle with depression, and eventually pursuing a college education.

I attended college in a wealthy community and observed rich people for the first time. I was a loner who delved into a rabbit hole of research and reading. I balanced my studies with raising my daughter and learning how to be a father. I didn't find too much interest in college so I started self-educating and engaged in more reading on topics of interest like psychedelics, consciousness, aliens, etc. Eventually, I returned to my hometown and attended parties, but my family's mindset differed greatly from my own. Consequently, I left home and went back to California where I experimented with psychedelics. This truly was one of the biggest game changers in my mindset. My ego died and my soul expanded.

After completing college and earning three associate degrees, I worked as a Lyft driver while also indulging in smoking weed. This period exposed me to new human experiences as I wandered around various parts of Southern California. I thoroughly loved engaging in conversations with random individuals on profound spiritual topics.

Furthermore, I enrolled in a computer programming Bootcamp and embraced the life of a nerd because for so long I had to hide that part of me from "friends".

During this time, I discovered that I had a brain aneurysm, which instilled panic and fear within me. As a result, my mindset underwent a transformation. I decided to return to my hometown so that my daughter could be raised in the presence of our family. To my disappointment, I realized that most of my friends had not changed since I left. Therefore, I initiated a podcast to address the issues in my community.

Additionally, I ventured into real estate investment and revitalized properties within the community. I practiced group economics to demonstrate the potential of pooling our resources for community development projects. Moreover, I established a non-profit organization and now run a boxing gym where I serve as a mentor to the youth. Currently, I am writing a book documenting my journey.

All of these events occurred between 2007 and 2022, from the ages of 18 to 33. Throughout these experiences, many of which I haven't described in writing, I noticed that upon returning home, my friends had remained unchanged. Some individuals had matured in their mindset, while others still possessed an immature outlook despite their adult bodies. They seemed to operate comfortably and unconsciously, akin to non-playable characters (NPCs) in a video game, adhering to the same routine for over a decade.

My primary objective upon returning home was to establish generational wealth so that my children and grandchildren would not have to endure poverty. Real estate became my focus, and I purchased my first property on the same block where I had spent my childhood.

In my mind, I was determined to set the example. Drawing upon the leadership and intense initiative skills I acquired from the Marine Corps, the newly found intellect gained through college and self-education, and the spiritually raised consciousness fostered by psychedelic experiences and diverse human interactions during my travels, I aspired to uplift my community in remarkable ways.

I firmly believed that by showcasing a clean environment with pristine buildings, I could elevate the emotions and spirits of the citizens around me. Armed with this conviction, I embarked on a mission to clean up a neglected block of the neighborhood. With sheer determination, I mowed, raked, and diligently picked up trash in front of the community.

As I worked, I couldn't help but notice some of the individuals on their porches, seemingly captivated by my actions. Even though they were consumed by their own struggles, perhaps even under the influence of drugs, they watched me with curious eyes, as if I were a living spectacle. Undeterred, I pressed on, recognizing that I held within me the power to inspire change.

Two days later, upon my return to the block, disappointment washed over me. The entire area was once again plagued by dirt and neglect. In that moment, a profound realization struck me like lightning. I understood that fixing the physical environment was only part of the equation. To truly uplift the community, I needed to elevate the mindset and consciousness of the people living there.

This epiphany became my defining moment. I recognized that some individuals possessed an aura brimming with self-illuminating sunshine, while others were shrouded in dark clouds of hopelessness. It became clear that I had to be my own ray of sunshine, shining brightly and steadfastly, while being mindful not to exhaust myself by pouring too much of my energy into others' darkness.

In America, there was a time when people turned to the Bible, the Koran, and the Torah. They lived by a set of agreed-upon commandments, learning life lessons and adhering to rules of conduct that benefited both themselves and their communities. Sadly, this standard of conduct is fading away. Today, the prevailing notion seems to be that of limitless freedom, an attitude that breeds lawlessness and a lack of accountability.

People are quick to cry, "Don't judge me!" when all we're trying to do is hold them accountable for the consequences of their poor decisions, which inevitably affect those around them. This realization led me to compile a book of personal quotes, life lessons, and experiences—a modern-day compendium of commandments and teachings to live by. It provides guidance and wisdom without the cryptic confusion often associated with traditional scriptures.

Let us embark on this journey together, armed with the lessons of leadership, intellect, and spiritual consciousness. By elevating our own frequencies of thought and action, we can inspire and uplift others, creating a ripple effect of positive change that will resonate throughout our communities and humanity as a whole. It begins with each of us, taking responsibility and striving for excellence in all that we do. Together, we can restore the sense of accountability and moral conduct that will bring about a brighter future for ourselves and the generations to come.

In the ceaseless battle of safeguarding our internal sunshine amidst life's storms, this book serves as our armor, uplifting our mindset and expanding our consciousness. Its transformative power extends beyond ourselves, positively impacting our family and community. With the grand mission of elevating humanity's collective consciousness, it empowers us to soar to new heights of personal growth and enlightenment. Embrace its wisdom, for within its pages lie the keys to unlocking brilliance and overcoming any dark clouds that may dim our eternal radiance.

*Get Home Safe means,
"I Love You", in a hostile environment.*

TABLE OF CONTENTS

The Phone Call	v
The Sun Versus the Cloud	viii
Love	1
Motivation	35
Experience	71
Mindset	129

GET HOME SAFE
* * *

Get home safe means, "I love you",
in a hostile environment. 🌙

The 4 P's of a Good Family Man (Outside Home) &
Woman (Inside Home) or Vice Versa
- Protect
- Provide
- Produce
- Preach 🌙

Life is fleeting. Seize the moment and reach out to those you hold dear. Engage in a sincere conversation, without expectation, and you will often find that the person on the other end needed that connection. ☀

LOVE
***

The masculine and feminine partnerships of society need to communicate how to have a good balance of the 4 P's to being a good family man or woman, see page 3. A balance of responsibility outside the home and a balance of responsibility inside the home. For example, in a traditional family setting, under natural law, the masculine partner would protect, provide, and produce outside of the home. While the feminine partner protects, provides and produces inside of the home. Both partners preach inside of the home to set the standard of conduct and traditions to their children inside the home. Nowadays, with the high cost of living, both partners tend to have to go outside the home to be able to provide for their families. This leaves the children susceptible inside the home to being raised by other sources of influence. In order for the household to not become out of balance a healthy sit down and jot down meeting between the two partners should become customary to ensure they are planning, protecting, and organizing a place of growth and peace for their family. 🌙

My loyalty remains strong, even if we don't communicate daily. If it was ever love, I still wish you well. ☀

If your children are not, all around, better versions of you, then you have failed them. 🌙

GET HOME SAFE
* * *

Physical appearance and style can initially attract attention, but true commitment, respect, understanding, and love come from getting to know someone on a deeper spiritual and mental level. Choose wisely and look for qualities that align with your expectations. ☀

It is easier to build up a child now than fix a broken adult later. 🌙

Your home should be your place of peace. 🌙

LOVE
***

Cherish those who come into your life and inspire you to be the best version of yourself. Those who bring peace, truth, healing, and help you discover your inner God are valuable. ☀

Women get charged during sex. Men get drained during sex. 🌙

Women care about a man's future; men care about a woman's past. 🌙

GET HOME SAFE
***

Building on a foundation of love often brings good fortune, while building on a foundation of hate can lead to disastrous outcomes. ☀

The best parents are the ones who remember what it was like to be a child, not the ones that force their child to act like an adult. 🌙

If my work, art, energy, or being has a positive impact on you, please don't give me all the credit. Acknowledge those who helped shape me into who I am today, including my mother, God, and the community around me. No one succeeds alone, and the love and guidance of others have played a significant role in my growth. ☀

LOVE
***

The word dull is in adult for a reason. As you age, most people lose their child-like sense of adventure. 🌙

Balance is key in fatherhood and marriage, prioritize your family over work success. Fathers are the core foundation their families will build on for generations. Your actions as a father and husband will shape the family's future and legacy. ☀

A daughter is a man's heart, a son is a man's legacy. 🌙

GET HOME SAFE
***

Material possessions will become meaningless in the long run, focus on leaving a strong family legacy. ☀

You can always tell the level of a man's thinking by how he treats his woman. 🌙

The moment my daughter was born, and we looked into each other's eyes for the first time, I felt a rush of energy from my head to my toes. Like our souls imprinted on one another and an eternal spiritual bond was formed. 🌙

LOVE

* * *

Love is often undervalued in our society, but it should be cherished. Love others unconditionally, regardless of their life circumstances, past mistakes, cultural background, religious beliefs, or any societal expectations they may not meet. Love openly and without reservation. ☀

Hospital births are unnatural. No other man should be the first one touching my child out the womb. The umbilical cord should not be cut in some sadistic ritual. It is my universal duty as a man to greet my newly born soul when they first arrive through the doorway of life, their mother's womb. 🌙

Personal growth is essential for being a better spouse and parent. ☀

GET HOME SAFE
* * *

A man's duty is to protect, provide, and produce outside his home in order to better prepare his children for the outside world. A woman's duty is to protect, provide, and produce inside her home. Instilling good habits, morals, and behavior so that her children will conduct themselves respectfully when they leave the nest. Both parents preach inside the home. This is the natural balance of a comfortable home. 🌙

It is a man's, as well as a woman's, duty from their thoughts to their actions to create an environment in their reality that allows everyone around them to flourish. 🌙

Your energy as you navigate through life as a father and husband will impact the entire family. Lead your family with love, positivity, discipline, and a commitment to excellence, and they will follow. ☀

LOVE
✳✳✳

Every good deed you do honors your ancestors. The more you honor your ancestors the stronger of a spiritual and electrical bond you will create with them. An energetic frequency, like a phone line, of communication will allow them to have easier access of communication to your mind. This will ensure your ancestors can protect and guide you from the spiritual realm even when you're walking down the path of life on your own. When you honor your ancestors you're rarely ever walking alone. Physically your alone, but spiritually your 100 deep.

Respect your DNA. Self-Love. 🌙

Be careful how much you work and neglect to spend quality time with your child, because that tablet will begin to take your place. In your place, it will begin to raise your child's mind and future. 🌙

Your children need love, attention, guidance, support, and understanding more than material items. ☀

GET HOME SAFE
***

Teach your children that social media should be used as a tool to build their brand and focus on their passion, and it's not to be used as a distraction. Like a hammer, I can build a house with it, or I can hit nails through my feet and keep myself stuck in one place for the rest of my life.

Honor those who push you to reach your full potential, motivate you to take action on your goals, support and build you up, provide healing and positivity, and instill confidence in your children. This is love, royalty, and a blessing. ☀

Recognize your generational trauma, that you acquired from your parents, and ensure you do not pass it on to your children. If you are aware of a trauma or flaw you're struggling with, be vulnerable, and express that flaw honestly about yourself to your children so they can become aware of what attributes and habits not to absorb from you.

LOVE

***

I firmly believe in the power of positive affirmations. Encourage children to believe in love, power, and positivity from an early age. Avoid negative comments and reinforce positive reinforcement and love daily. ☀

You should not beat your children, but we do them an injustice by not lightly spanking muscle memory into them to ensure they understand physical consequences for their poor actions. When you release them into the world, the world will punch them in the face and not give a fuck about their tears. Prep your child to have the awareness to assess a visible threat, whether it's physically, mentally, or emotionally, and to have a solution-based mindset to figure out a plan of action to deal with it. This will pay them back greatly by helping them avoid long-term repercussions from unaware, cowardly, or naive decision making. 🌙

Saying I love you doesn't mean anything if there is no action before or after the words are spoken. 🌙

GET HOME SAFE
***

A genuine man embodies discipline, selflessness, and follows through on his promises. He treats everyone with respect, regardless of their background. A genuine man finds fulfillment in assisting and supporting others and is always striving to expand his knowledge. He conducts himself with honesty and honor, and treats the women in his life with dignity, as they reflect on him. ☀

If your child isn't a better version of you in every single way, you have failed them. You should be expressing and explaining the areas of life you messed up at to ensure they don't make the same mistake. If they do, it's at a much earlier age of their life than you were when you made that mistake. This helps to elevate and advance your family bloodline. 🌙

My goal is to build a life with a supportive spouse, raise a family in a beautiful home with a white picket fence, and gather with friends for barbecues and card games, reminiscing about our journey. ☀

LOVE

***

Patience and love are cousins. 🌙

Ghosting mother fuckers who throw you off your life path is a form of self-love. 🌙

Words such as "can't", "won't", and "unable" should not be used when speaking to children. If a child expresses doubt about their ability to complete a task, encourage them to give it a try and believe in their ability. Your role is to instill confidence and courage in them to overcome any challenges and pursue their dreams. ☀

GET HOME SAFE
* * *

No matter how infatuated you are with someone, a certain level of privacy is necessary to maintain that infatuated spark of mystery. Walking in on someone taking a shit can quickly destroy the deepest of intimacy.

🌙

Children are more likely to become what you show them than become what you tell them. Telling isn't teaching.

🌙

Before moving on to the next page, reach out to someone and have a genuine conversation. Call your grandparents, friends, family, or old co-worker and offer positive reinforcement. Most of the time, you'll realize they needed that conversation, and your gesture can make a big impact. ☀

LOVE
***

The burning passion to provide for someone you love can be exhausting. A man's drive to hustle for his family may lead to his burnout. We have a hard time taking off the superhero uniform for our family. This will eventually lead to feeling drained, irritable, and having outbursts. It's imperative for us to know when to rest, not only physically, but mentally. Even if you're resting, but mentally worried about not getting shit done, you will never feel fully recharged. This is why it is so necessary and wise for a man to choose a woman who heals and creates a peaceful environment to come home to. 🌙

Before you become romantic with someone, ensure you evaluate their mindset in these specific areas of self: mental, emotional, spiritual, physical, financial, intellectual, and adventure. Then, ask them to prioritize those issues in their lives from most important to least. It's okay if they are not in the same order as you. Writing it down shows visual awareness of where each other needs to help balance the other. 🌙

GET HOME SAFE
***

Mom, I wish you were still here. Your spirit pushes me forward every time I fall. Every time I consider giving up, I feel you telling me to keep going. I'm dedicating my work, clothing, studies, and knowledge-seeking to you. I'm doing my best to get my grandma a house and I want everyone to feel the positivity, love, and peace I'm spreading through my brand and motivational videos. I believe in all those who are up late filling out job applications, single mothers struggling to make ends meet, and them children with big dreams. My brand will always be about positivity, love, and peace. Thank you to those who believe in me and support me. And most of all, thank you, Mom, for believing in me. I'll see you soon. ☀

Sitting in the house while you're in one room and your child is in another isn't being a father/mother. Showing up to their band concert even though you know it's not going to be pleasant to the ears but it's going to light up their soul when they see you is being a father/mother.

LOVE
***

Your first bath was done by someone. Your last bath will be done by someone. Do not walk around with pride and arrogance or your last bath won't be done by someone who loves you. 🌙

If all my business ventures fail, but I have inspired someone to be fearless in their own journey to success, I will be satisfied. If I have raised my children with a pure heart and taught them the principles instilled in me by my mother, and they go on to inspire others, I will be satisfied. ☀

My daughter's mother is my family, regardless if we are in a relationship or not. We created a child. It is our duty to our child to create a loving space when we encounter one another, guide them through obstacles by giving both masculine and feminine point of views, and create blissful memories together even if we both have significant others. 🌙

GET HOME SAFE
***

Respect and cherish your mothers, educate your sisters, guide, and protect your daughters, and honor your wife. These women are phenomenal, they are works of art, and they are the reason for every human on earth. We all originate from their care, love, and nurturing. The greatest lesson I have learned from the women in my life is the power of the heart and managing one's emotions. A king is nothing without the guidance of his surrounding queens. ☀

The energy of the chef who cooks your food matters. Eat a meal from your loving wife or have grandmas home cooking. Then go try some synthetic fast food and let me know how you feel afterwards. 🌙

Street dudes, consider making your family and children proud by providing them with happiness, independence, love, and wisdom for future success, rather than only gaining recognition on the block. ☀

LOVE

***

Regardless if I'm with my daughter's mother or not, we still do family shit together all the time. Even though we see other people, we still make an effort to do shit as a family. It's extremely beneficial for our daughter's future, in how she conducts herself and how she communicates with others, for her to see her parents working together and getting along. 🌙

The best present you can give me is for you to cultivate self-love, self-reliance, and independent thinking. ☀

A good wife with graceful goddess energy can put the hardest working man, who is extremely stressed, immediately at peace. 🌙

GET HOME SAFE
***

There are certain roles in life that cannot be neglected, like being a good brother, son, grandson, and eventually a father. As a man, your duty is to take care of your family as long as you live. ☀

I taught my daughter to stand up for herself. I wasn't ready when she stood up to me. 🌙

As members of a family, it is our responsibility to guide and shape the next generation, whether it's our own children or younger family members. Instead of relying on external influences and teachers, let us take the initiative to steer our loved ones in the right direction. Our focus should be on investing in them, as growth is a lifelong process. The choices we make now will determine their future and whether they will be influenced by the world or by us. ☀

LOVE
***

A gentle woman's touch can turn a house into a home. 🌙

When saying goodbye to someone, the next most important thing after expressing love is to wish them a safe return home. Any day that ends with you being home safely is a good day. ☀

It's your duty to heal, to ensure you stop taking your traumas and triggers out on those you love. 🌙

GET HOME SAFE
***

Achieving big milestones or winning major events every day is not necessary for success. Focus on acting from a place of love and kindness towards others and consider each day a success if you accomplished this. ☀

When you're in a relationship, saying shit doesn't hold any weight long term. Only doing shit does. 🌙

External compliments are appreciated, but the greatest recognition is for the qualities of your heart, mind, and soul. ☀

LOVE

***

Some people can't comprehend how to have a healthy co-parenting relationship. How to still have a healthy family bond even if the parents aren't together. They're still focused on why the relationship didn't work out. Selfishly bitter, refusing to give their child a peaceful companionship with the other parent. In turn, they never show their children how to communicate in a healthy manner when something doesn't go their way. Passing down generational curses that they could have healed within themselves. 🌙

Fatherhood should be your top priority in life, as it will have the greatest impact on your life and future generations. ☀

GET HOME SAFE
***

Telling your friend to, *"Get Home Safe"*, is one of the rare gestures of affection men show one another. 🌙

Discipline is the first step of self-love. 🌙

Lead your family by breaking free from negative patterns and expectations, setting a high bar for future generations to follow. ☀

LOVE
***

A baby becomes a boy because of the mother.
A boy becomes a man because of the father. 🌙

The world needs dangerously intelligent men, their
aggressive form of love keeps the evil men at bay. 🌙

Treat everyone, regardless of their impact on your life,
with love and respect. Be ethical and do the right thing,
even when no one is watching. ☀

GET HOME SAFE
***

Sometimes the best medicine is a listening ear. 🌙

The moment my daughter was born, and we locked eyes for the first time, I felt a rush of energy flow from the top of my head to the bottom of my feet. Our auras imprinted on one another, and I knew that this was the first time I felt true unconditional love. 🌙

I strive to be an embodiment of the message that you can heal from past traumas and live with a loving heart, open mind, gentle spirit, and a desire to serve others. ☀

LOVE

***

If you elevate your children, you can pamper your grandchildren. If you pamper your children, you will have to elevate your grandchildren. 🌙

Dating should be renamed to interviewing. 🌙

When you're feeling uncertain or like giving up, close your eyes and think of someone you love deeply. Remember those who bring light and peace to your heart, and those who believe in you and would be disappointed if you gave up. Let their love fuel your determination to keep going. ☀

GET HOME SAFE
***

Evaluate and assess your future partner during the dating process. It could be the best or worst decision you ever make. 🌙

If they give you peace, give them your time. 🌙

Self-love involves introspection and self-awareness, as well as making deliberate efforts to become the best version of yourself while staying humble and kind to others. It's okay to make mistakes, but self-love involves acknowledging, accepting, and learning from them. ☀

LOVE
***

Stop falling into lust and start rising into love. Lust is a short-term investment; love is a long-term investment. 🌙

Women who are raised in a fatherless home have a high probability of becoming two types of women. They either become too accessible to men, attention seeking. Looking for masculine acceptance and allowing men to come in and out of their life without evaluating the moral character of that man before allowing them access. Or they become extremely aggressive towards men because of the lack of healthy masculine guidance in their past, and this makes them hostile communicators. As well as, emotionally draining women to be in a relationship with.
A mature well-mannered father with a good moral character who is stern when necessary is obligatory for our daughters to grow into respectable young women. If no father can be found, a masculine mentor is necessary in their youth. 🌙

GET HOME SAFE
***

My goal is to create financial stability for my family for generations to come, but my soul mission is even more important to me. If I can use my platform to spread messages of love, peace, and unity, and help heal the world, that is my true identity and purpose. ☀

Let go of sex when starting a relationship. Sex shouldn't be the capital letter at the beginning of the sentence to start your relationship, it should be the exclamation point at the end of the sentence to cap off the relationship. 🌙

What will you leave your children? How about happiness, unity, life insurance, family trust, assets, wisdom, skill sets, financial literacy, spiritual intuitiveness, connection with nature, and respect for their ancestors. If they are stuck in a survival state of consciousness, don't expect your future blood line to evolve past its current generational curses. 🌙

MOTIVATION
***

Stay Focused. THAT'S THE UNSPOKEN WAR. Don't give them your mind. 🌙

Perfection is not a pre-requisite for inspiring others. It is your ability to overcome imperfections that serves as a source of inspiration ☀

The true hell is when the person you are meets the person you could have been. 🌙

GET HOME SAFE
***

Success requires persistence. You may face rejections, failures, and lack of support from those close to you, but all successful stories share one common trait: persistence.

Waiting for "the right time" will never happen, so take a bold step forward. Great achievements come from those who pursue their dreams. ☀

Your procrastination will slit the throat of your motivation before you can reach your destination. 🌙

MOTIVATION
***

War does not measure the strength of a man. War measures the will of a man. 🌙

In all scriptures detailing success or life, one common denominator remains constant: persistence. The key to victory is never quitting. ☀

It is better to conquer the fear of doubt than to die with regret. 🌙

GET HOME SAFE

***

Adhere to your principles and vision while promoting your brand, product, and price. Some may unfollow, dislike your drive, or be inspired, but either way, business will be conducted. ☀

True growth happens when you are willing to face challenges and discomfort without being overwhelmed by fear. Your comfort zone will not bring you the success you seek. ☀

MOTIVATION
***

Execution breeds effort, effort breeds execution. 🌙

Achieving success requires a combination of a positive mindset and action. Both courage and self-belief are necessary to start, while discipline and perseverance are crucial in overcoming any challenges that arise along the way. This formula remains constant in any pursuit of success. Success requires a combination of a positive mindset and action. You need to have both confidence and self-belief to start, and the discipline and determination to overcome any obstacles and challenges that arise during the journey. This is the key to success every time. ☀

That voice in your head can make or break your future. Control it. 🌙

GET HOME SAFE
＊＊＊

Let go of the person you were yesterday so you can grow tomorrow. 🌙

The future can be predicted by examining one's thoughts, actions, and habits. By having productive thoughts, actions, and habits, one will experience positive outcomes. Your personal story is shaped by what you allow into your mind, your daily routines, and your actions. Take control and create your own reality. ☀

We all cross a path where we must decide to do what is right or what is easy. 🌙

MOTIVATION

***

Fighters face great peril every time they step into the ring. They risk being knocked down and even losing their lives. But we have also seen countless stories of fighters who, even when they fell, got back up, regained their composure, rethought their strategy, and kept pushing forward. Their determination and bravery shines through. The fight is never over until the final bell sounds. Keep pushing forward. ☀

When you're around people who aren't aligned with your personal destiny, your soul becomes irritated and exhausted. 🌙

Don't be so hard on yourself" is a phrase that's been said to me many times by others. However, it doesn't affect me because they can't truly comprehend the drive, I have to reach my goals. No one can understand the fire that burns within you like you do. It's important to take breaks for growth, but never let that passion fade. Don't let anyone else dull the flame inside you. ☀

GET HOME SAFE
***

Treat your energy like money, invest it where you know you're going to get a return. 🌙

The greats separate themselves by pushing through the tough days. They work even when they're tired, uninspired, and haven't seen progress. That's when true character is displayed. ☀

My generation no longer gives a fuck about a job. We give a fuck about ownership. 🌙

MOTIVATION
* * *

Adversity is an opportunity to display our skills, knowledge, and self-belief. Embrace it, smile through it, and become better because of it. ☀

A rich man with a broken soul will become envious of a poor man with a strong aura. 🌙

Have patience for the end goal but be impatient in the actions required to reach it. Take ownership of your actions, evaluate yourself honestly, and hold yourself accountable. ☀

GET HOME SAFE

* * *

When the right people water you, you flow differently.

To reach our goals and become the best version of ourselves, we must build a daily system that supports our progress. This means evaluating our habits and eliminating those that steer us away from our goals, while embracing new ones. ☀

Start your own business and start hiring your children. Start learning to legally protect your families future assets with trusts and creating your own family life insurance bank so you can pass them down. This is how you create generational wealth. By creating new traditions and financial standards within your family. This begins the process of breaking your families generational curses of poverty and financial illiteracy.

MOTIVATION
***

Take the chance and dare to risk it all, rather than play it safe. ☀

Don't build wealth for your children, build wealth with your children. 🌙

Every man in difficult circumstances should strive to be the one who "made it" for his entire family. ☀

GET HOME SAFE
***

A billionaire once said that if you don't show your children the importance of building and maintaining wealth, they will become spoiled and entitled. The second or third generation after you will lose everything in their lifetime that you worked for in your lifetime. Create strong family principles, traditions, and easy to learn business practices, and pass them down. 🌙

Successful people make mistakes. Don't label yourself based on your past mistakes, instead focus on growing and moving forward. ☀

Don't be afraid of being a copycat just copy the right cat. You don't have to recreate the wheel when you find the right mentor who's already made one before. 🌙

MOTIVATION
* * *

Living a purposeful life comes with challenges and obstacles. Be proud when you face difficulties and don't give in, this sets you apart from the majority. ☀

The right mentor could change your life overnight. 🌙

What if someone told you they knew you only had ten more years left? What if someone told you that you'll only have five more opportunities to spend thanksgiving with your family? What if someone said you only have ten more times to take your kids to the park? What if you only had five more chances to tell your loved ones you love them? Would you appreciate life differently? Would you see life from a different perspective? Don't take this thing called life for granted. Pick up the phone, reach out, make the effort because you can't get the time back. Love each day and express your love. Keep the family close as we only get one shot in life. There is no rewind button. No do over. Don't ignore your souls calling, your true purpose, your goals or just spending precious moments with your loved ones. ☀

GET HOME SAFE
***

Stop criticizing yourself and letting external forces make you feel unworthy. Spend the next half-year affirming your worth, envisioning yourself deserving of all you desire, and putting in the effort. Observe the transformation. ☀

Network. Knowing the right people with their foot already in certain doors makes it easier for you to find opportunities to raise your net worth. 🌙

Embrace challenges as growth opportunities, understanding that they are all part of your journey to fulfill your purpose. ☀

MOTIVATION

***

If you don't like who you currently are and have a vision of who you want to be, write down three things you need to learn or do to get there on a post-it note. Put it right in front of your face next to your bed, so when you wake up, you know what the plan of the day is. Once you complete those three tasks, write down the next three things to learn and do. You gently start to create new habits and focus towards who you want to be, so you're not sitting around fantasizing about who you could have been. Think, and have a plan, but don't think and get lost in the what-ifs or fear of failure. Failure is good, it means you're trying. Taking action will turn it from a fantasy in your mind to a reality in your life. 🌙

When faced with challenges, view them as opportunities for growth and embrace the lessons they bring. Everything happens for a reason and with determination, you can overcome obstacles. ☀

A stagnant life stuck in your comfort zone inevitably leads to you getting older every year and dying. Stepping out of your comfort zone inevitably leads you to becoming a newer version every year and transcending.

🌙

GET HOME SAFE
***

We are constantly at war, but we don't see it anymore because no bombs are dropping. Instead, the silent bombs of economy, education, entertainment, labor, law, social media, algorithms, medicine, music, pharmaceuticals, politics, religion, sex, and war drop on us every second of our lives. We are at war economically because the education system teaches us nothing about financial literacy. Only the rich get to go to private schools and acquire that information at a young age. The century old education system doesn't prepare a modern-day curriculum for the fast-evolving job market, especially in tech. Why is it that coding is taught in public schools in India but rarely seen in American classes? The entertainment industry promotes murder music, hyper sexuality is forced on to our children, social media stealing the attention and focus of everyday people allowing their gift of life to waste away watching cat videos. Celebrities use their influence to lower the moral standards and principles in the family household. Labor intensifies as the demand for productivity increases, but wages stay the same. The law is written in a language the common man can't even understand. The medical industry is filled with doctors who aren't natural healers but synthetic pharmaceutical distributors. Politicians are lobbied and paid for, so they are not operating on a moral compass that benefits the collective consciousness of humanity.

MOTIVATION
* * *

Religion divides our focus of consciousness, never allowing humanity to fully merge into one collective state of consciousness focused on the single mission of evolving and healing humanity spiritually. There are never ending wars to benefit corporate greed, malevolent political agendas, and the military industrial complex. It almost seems like the people in power aren't even human. With all these odds stacked against us...We. Still. Fight. Back. 🌙

GET HOME SAFE
***

If you only push yourself to work hard on the days you feel good, you won't accomplish much. Pursuing impossible dreams requires an impossible work ethic. I learned this through my own experiences and mistakes and strive to give 110% effort every day, even on my worst days, which is what great individuals do. ☀

If I ever, did you a favor or showed you love, you don't owe me anything in return. Love is unconditional. ☀

Most young men and women are not mentally equipped to pursue their passion after high school, let alone financially equipped. I wasn't. So, one day, I got really high, read a lot of books, listened to lectures, paid for mentors, and taught myself. 🌙

You are closer to your goals now than when you started. Don't give up. Take a break, reevaluate, and keep moving forward. ☀

MOTIVATION

***

Don't waste your energy on revenge. Level up and forget they existed. 🌙

The average person adapts to the world around them, but the exceptional person persists in trying to shape the world to their vision. All progress depends on these exceptional individuals. ☀

The real new year starts the first day of spring when Earth's energy starts to rise. Start your resolutions when the plants start to grow with you, so your goals—those you want to manifest—begin to grow serendipitously with the earth. 🌙

GET HOME SAFE
***

Take control of your life and don't let it control you. Society is not designed to help you succeed and build a legacy for your family, so it's up to you to create, build, plan, and unlearn society's norms of complacency. Think about the wisdom, wealth, and legacy you want to leave behind. ☀

An L isn't a loss, it's a lesson. 🌙

Life is a risk, so why not bet on yourself and your kids? ☀

MOTIVATION
***

You cannot work your way to wealth. You must invest your way to wealth. 🌙

Being self-made requires unwavering dedication and sacrifice, leaving no room for excuses in pursuing your goals and dreams. ☀

Take responsibility for your own actions. Invest in a dry erase board, attach it in a prominent location in your room with command strips, and fill it with both short- and long-term goals. Seeing the board each day will remind you of the progress you have (or haven't) made and motivate you to take small steps towards crossing items off the list. ☀

Who will you learn from if you're the smartest person in the room? 🌙

GET HOME SAFE
***

The two biggest mistakes in life are not giving it your all and not starting at all. ☀

How do you master standing up to your fears? You have to pretend to be fearless. 🌙

Challenges and negativity are simply opportunities for me to rise and grow further. ☀

MOTIVATION
✳ ✳ ✳

If you still have that childlike sense of adventure in you, you're a fucking beast. This system tries daily to destroy that sparkle for life that was in everyone's eyes the moment they were born. 🌙

Success requires not knowing it all but being what most lack: consistency and discipline. ☀

Emotion stands for energy in motion. Your energy is the real currency. Money is what they pay you for your energy, that's how valuable it is. They had to create a physical monetary system to pay for your energy. Your existence is the spiritual gold of the universe. Respect it. 🌙

GET HOME SAFE
***

Your journey may inspire others, so don't give up or lose focus, stay true to your path, and keep moving forward.

We become successful because we were willing to get up and fail. 🌙

Embracing failure and rejection transforms you into a relentless machine. ☀

MOTIVATION
***

Wake up and get ready to fail. That's how you become successful. 🌙

The most meaningful human act is to inspire others, according to Nip. Inspiration should be the determining factor of success, even if not everyone understands this viewpoint. ☀

If you're a god, you're supposed to teach. 🌙

GET HOME SAFE
***

God will not inquire about the amount of money I earned or the respect I received, but rather, the number of lives I positively impacted and the hearts I changed for the better. ☀

Sometimes an L in the physical realm is a W in the spiritual realm. 🌙

Despite the setbacks I've encountered, I view them as motivation to keep pushing forward. ☀

MOTIVATION
✱✱✱

Eternity frightens the thoughts of man and whether or not his legacy will echo for the entirety of eternity's existence. 🌙

When everything else fails, focus on your grind, and hustle and never lose sight of why you started and the positive impact it will have on your family and the world. ☀

When undergoing personal transformation, there will be those who try to pull you back into your comfort zone. Don't become a victim of complacency, push past the obstacles, and strive towards reaching your highest potential. A beautiful outcome awaits you on the other side of these challenges. ☀

People only remember the names of those who stood courageously against what everyone else feared. 🌙

GET HOME SAFE
* * *

Focus on your goals and lay the foundation for what you want to achieve. Take it one day at a time and keep pushing forward. Remember, it's a marathon, not a sprint. ☀

You're one good decision away from being where you want. Keep making them daily. 🌙

When you work hard, you master your skill set. When you master your skillsets, you acquire more responsibility. When you're lazy, you lose what you once mastered. When you lose that ability, you will no longer be trusted with responsibilities. 🌙

MOTIVATION
* * *

A dream is nothing without action. ☀

Belief is key to reaching your potential. Obstacles are opportunities to test your resolve and to push past them, you need to have faith in yourself and your abilities. You have what it takes to overcome any challenges and reach your goals. I have confidence in you. ☀

Why be sorry? Be better. 🌙

GET HOME SAFE
***

Motivational memes, quotes, and talk alone won't achieve your dreams. You need to take action and have faith in your goals to make them a reality. Nobody else will do it for you! ☀

There is no bigger shame than to be useless. 🌙

To my brother or sister reading this, know that this journey won't be easy, but don't let self-doubt or tears stop you. Embrace lessons and keep pushing towards the finish line, knowing that I'm here to support you. ☀

MOTIVATION
***

There are places of poverty amongst all races, cities, and villages where it's become a tradition of stagnant misery to project their internal anger and disappointment of themselves on to others. Do not allow their dark clouds to block out your sunlight. 🌙

Whenever someone asks me how I am, I reply that I am blessed. Even if I may be facing some challenges at the moment, I understand that my blessings always outweigh my struggles. Instead of complaining, I focus on moving forward. ☀

You're not a winner because you tried. You become a winner because you trained. 🌙

GET HOME SAFE
***

You never fail when you try, you only fail when fear stops you from trying. 🌙

Don't wait for a guide to show you the way. You can't anticipate setbacks, failures, victories, support, or opposition, but take the leap with the confidence that you're on the right track. ☀

Walk into the darkness. That's where you develop in all areas of your life. They say you need to find the light at the end of tunnel. That's false. A real master becomes the light to guide others through the tunnel. Stars do not exist when the sun is out. We need the darkness. Go flourish in it. 🌙

MOTIVATION
***

Are you breathing? Is your body able to function? Are you still capable of critical thinking? Yes. Then you're good. Get up. Write down your goals. Make a step-by-step checklist. Accomplish a couple of those tasks a day and let the journey begin. Somewhere along the way, years later, someone is going to need your help because they are where you were. Will you be a teacher at that time because you stepped into your journey? Or are you going to stay in your comfort zone, forever a student and follower? 🌙

You become very powerful when you learn to think, plan, organize, travel, and conquer things on your own. 🌙

To achieve extraordinary results, you need to set bold goals that others can't imagine. Have unwavering self-belief and discipline to reach those targets. ☀

Simply having an interest in something is not enough to achieve success. Study those who have achieved seemingly impossible goals and understand that they were obsessed, not just interested. Decide if you want to be average or great. ☀

GET HOME SAFE
* * *

Embrace challenges and embrace the doubt. I grew the most as a person when I faced adversity and emerged stronger, despite the anxiety it caused. To achieve extreme success, you need to have unwavering belief in yourself, as the journey will test you. But when you persevere, life on the other side is beautiful. ☀

80% of success is mindset and attitude, while the remaining 20% is skill set. ☀

The best version of yourself emerges when you are challenged, not when you are comfortable. Discover your true potential when facing adversity and anxiety. ☀

True success is persistence in the face of repeated failure without losing self-belief. ☀

MOTIVATION
✶ ✶ ✶

Remember the joy of playing as a child when the Earth was your playground? Just because you've grown into an adult doesn't mean that should change. Take a moment to relax, breathe, and truly appreciate the beautiful sights along your journey. 🌙

Embrace being unique and not fitting in. Not everything has to be understood by others. Your goals don't require validation from those around you. Overcome doubt, learn from mistakes and failures, and remain confident in your vision. ☀

Take action on your ideas even when you don't feel fully prepared. Do your research, put in the work, and have good intentions, and you'll see a shift in your reality. Place yourself in unfamiliar situations, start that business, give that presentation, and do something that makes you uncomfortable. When others try to hold you back with their insecurities, prove them wrong by succeeding. ☀

EXPERIENCE
✳ ✳ ✳

Once as a manager in Philadelphia we had a tremendous workload and I had limited staff available to assist. We got through the day working united and I sat them down and simply thanked them for their efforts. One replied it's been so long since anyone thanked me ever. The remainder of the team agreed. This taught me to never underestimate the power of positive reinforcement and recognizing the good in others. A simple thank you can go a long way. Leaders often focus on what needs to be improved, but we also need to appreciate and acknowledge what's being done well. ☀

Leaving my hometown immediately after high school saved my life. 🌙

The military confirmed to me that humanity is a tribal species. We flourish collectively when we're surrounded by others who are focused on the same goal. 🌙

Having meaningful conversations with the right people can have a transformative impact and stimulate mental growth, while engaging in aimless gossip is a waste of time. Avoid mistaking one for the other. ☀

GET HOME SAFE

* * *

All politicians should have to do an ayahuasca ritual. 🌙

Growing up with a stepdad who then left us in a fatherless home with a mother working 12-hour shifts at the hospital left me alone a lot in my teenage years. The streets, hip hop, movies, local gangsters, music, television, and porn raised and developed my mind. A chip on my shoulder developed, as I constantly tried to prove myself as a man. As rebellious as I was, I didn't realize that I needed a man in my life until my drill instructor at bootcamp told me he was proud of me, and I started crying. 🌙

Investing time in your parents or grandparents will never bring regret, but failing to do so will always leave you with remorse. This comes from personal experience. ☀

EXPERIENCE

* * *

A common regret in life is not reaching out to others. Life is short, so reach out to your support network, old friends, and positive experiences. You never know who needs a call or text with love and positivity. ☀

I have faced hardships in my life, including being betrayed by those I trusted, but I have learned valuable lessons from these experiences and never looked back. Even though my old home with my momma always on the other side to greet me and the comfort it once provided are gone, I have grown from my struggles and moved forward. ☀

Young teenage boys will grow a huge desire to go through a masculine ritual of approval. They want to prove themselves as a man. If a man or mentor is not present to guide them, the influence of the streets, mainstream promotion of murder music, and naivety of certain social media influencers will. They will grow a distasteful desire to hurt or shoot anyone in their path because they believe that is what makes them a man. 🌙

GET HOME SAFE
***

A wide-eyed child whose hard-working single mother elevated him to a suburban kid. A suburban kid who wanted to become a man, so he joined the Marines. A Marine who challenged authority and became a rebellious leader. A leader of men, but a womanizer who becomes a father to a daughter. A father, veteran, and leader who is now passionately focused on elevating his family, his community, and humanity. Time and experience constantly mold and recreate you. 🌙

Making the same mistake more than once is not an error, it is a deliberate choice. ☀

If you were rebellious and challenged authority, get ready for your children to challenge your authority. You can either yell and scream at them, trying to force them into submission, which will make them resentful toward you. Alternatively, you can communicate your reasoning in immense detail for them to comprehend and understand your way of doing things. They may agree and conform, or they may become curious and continue questioning to the point where they might teach you something about yourself and show you that you're the one who may need to change. 🌙

EXPERIENCE

✱ ✱ ✱

Social media can be incredibly useful when utilized for the right purposes. Many leading thinkers and entrepreneurs share their insights and knowledge on the platform. By following them, you gain access to this valuable information. By engaging deeply, the algorithm will also direct you towards like-minded individuals. ☀

A man or woman with discipline is like a hot air balloon maneuvering through the air to his desired destination. A man or woman without discipline is like those birthday balloons someone accidentally let go of into the air being pushed around wherever the wind blows. 🌙

When pursuing your purpose, you will face moments of fear and uncertainty, but these are signs that you are on the right path. ☀

GET HOME SAFE
* * *

The saddest humans on earth are usually people pleasers trying to make everyone happy. It is an impossible mission.

Being known for love and kindness brings good things, as people speak well of you even when you're not around.

☀

As life flows, we hit these midlife crisis points, looking for a savior to give us direction. Sometimes, they come, and sometimes they don't. If you keep waiting hopelessly for someone to save you, you will avoid your destiny until they arrive. When you search, find, feel, absorb, and upload your life's purpose, you begin to understand that there will be days, months, and even years of loneliness to achieve the desired destination. Master the art of being alone so your future doesn't hinge on the dependency of other people's actions to accomplish your goals.

EXPERIENCE

***

The value of a moment is only realized when it becomes a memory. We can look back on trips through photos and videos, but we can never fully experience the present again. So, cherish every moment and stay fully present.

The peace of being alone can become so addicting that you become complacent in it, avoiding the necessary chaos you must endure to sharpen your skills and wits in order to evolve and ascend your current level of consciousness. Stagnant water creates mold, and the same will happen to your mind if you become complacent in peace. 🌙

Not everyone who smiles is truly happy, and even those who appear to be shining bright may be carrying deep pain and trauma. Be kind and lead with love, as a single act of kindness can change someone's outlook on life. Be mindful of your interactions and manage your emotions during conflicts, as most disagreements are not worth the fight. ☀

GET HOME SAFE
***

When you fail, you either continue to take action or you don't. When you take action, you gain knowledge. When you gain knowledge, you adjust. When you adjust, you progress. When you progress, you transform your habits. When you transform your habits, you overcome outdated thinking. When you overcome outdated thinking, you encounter new opportunities. When you encounter new opportunities, you face unfamiliar situations. When you face unfamiliar situations, you test your limits. When you test your limits, you push yourself to grow. When you push yourself to grow, you transform into a better version of yourself. Repeat. Go fail. 🌙

The people you surround yourself with have a big impact on your life. Choose those who bring out the best in you, challenge you, and hold you accountable. Avoid those who limit your potential and bring excuses. Seek out those who inspire you, such as mentors, coaches, therapists, or those who believe in your greatness. Your community is essential to your growth and success. "It takes a village." ☀

In a society that praises material obsession, the spiritual healers get the least recognition. 🌙

EXPERIENCE
* * *

The journey of life is often filled with uncertainty and unanswered questions. You may feel lost and confused at times, but it's important to remember that you are closer to your destination than where you started. Trust that you are growing, healing, and moving in the right direction, even if you don't fully understand every step.

The Marine Corps is a brotherhood of misfits. 🌙

Don't let others' opinions and online personas shape your self-perception. Many people only showcase their highlights and successes on social media, leading to unrealistic comparisons and a skewed understanding of reality. Remember that there are people who have seen you at your worst and still love and accept you for who you are. Let their love and support be the foundation of your self-perception, not the judgment of others. You are amazing as you are. ☀

GET HOME SAFE
***

I send spirits, not bullets. 🌙

True leaders lead by example, creating a clear vision that inspires and motivates those around them. ☀

When God's trying to tell you something, He speaks through energy. Be still. Breathe, and tap into the inner energy patterns of yourself. Decipher the intuitive uploads into your mind. Some come from emotional impulse, fear, and the cravings of the five senses. Eat electrical food that grows from God's creation, Earth, so your body can radiate at a higher frequency, and resist the desires of the 7 deadly sins. When you operate on a high set of principles and aren't easily influenced, it becomes much easier to hear when God and your ancestors are speaking to you. 🌙

Stay indifferent to challenges and maintain calm in the face of adversity. Control your emotions and energy, even when the game is testing you. Despite losing my mother, being broke, sleeping on my grandmother's couch, and feeling heartbroken and alone, I've stuck to my beliefs and put out positive energy. You'll see how things fall into place when you do. ☀

EXPERIENCE
***

Equanimity is crucial for managing emotions in tough situations. As a leader, parent, or head of the household, it's essential to cultivate this skill so those who depend on you will feel calm and secure during challenging moments. ☀

Veterans feel lost after the military because they miss the village lifestyle they lived in while in the military. Men need to be in a pack of strong and courageous men to operate at their peak. 🌙

Growing up in tough circumstances, I feel a sense of responsibility to change the future for the next generation. We celebrate negative things like rap beef and gossip but complain about living in a war zone. Let's eliminate negativity from our minds and start creating change. ☀

A strong man encompasses both being a gentle emotional master and a savage warrior, using each trait as needed with ease. ☀

GET HOME SAFE
* * *

A cold shower will momentarily cure anxiety and depression immediately. 🌙

Not every older gentleman is an "OG". Experience may be the best teacher, but it's up to us to distinguish between those who have gained wisdom from their experiences and those who pass on negativity and harm. A true "OG" is one who inspires and serves as a positive example, even in adverse circumstances. ☀

Depression is a serious issue, but the feeling of overcoming it is beyond words. Don't let difficult times bring you down. Overcome your mind, and you can overcome anything life throws at you. As Nipsey Hussle said, "never let a hard time humble you". ☀

If you woke up negative, go back to bed. If that's not an option, take an ice-cold shower and ensure the water touches every part of your body, especially your spine, face, and head. 🌙

- 83 -

EXPERIENCE
***

This book is meant to capture my values, wisdom, and knowledge in written form, without the typical book elements of characters and plot. It serves as a guide for future generations of my family when I am no longer able to share my thoughts and out of energy. The ultimate goal is to leave a legacy. ☀

Be aware of the jealous traits coming from your family and friends. 🌙

Embrace challenges as growth opportunities, understanding that they are all part of your journey to fulfill your purpose. ☀

You can forgive someone without restoring the bond. 🌙

I was told in high school that I'd end up dead or in jail if I continued down a certain path, but now I'm here to serve as an example that your past doesn't determine your future. Inspiring others wasn't originally on my plan, but here I am. ☀

GET HOME SAFE
***

When you take the red pill and become Neo from *The Matrix*, you become aware of the current systems malevolent agenda against the conscious evolution and spiritual enlightenment of humanity. You begin speaking your mind on topics that consist of uncomfortable truths. This will usually disrupt the current narrative and level of consciousness that people around you are operating on. They can't predict what you are going to say next. They start suffering from cognitive dissonance. Your information is disrupting their current indoctrinated programming and traditions. They then begin to glitch. They become docile, predictable, and programmable—easy to read. They will eventually become uncomfortable with you because your presence makes them question their current state of existence. They will either disregard their current programming and elevate with you or transform into Agent Smiths. Continuously trying to convince you you're wrong in order to protect their comfort with the current system and their reality. 🌙

Being honest and open about one's flaws, insecurities, and mistakes is the only way to build genuine partnerships. When you show vulnerability and wear your heart on your sleeve, you become unstoppable and leave a lasting impact on others. ☀

EXPERIENCE

***

In high school I grew up with black, Hispanic, and white kids. I also hung out with the jocks, goths, hood gangstas, preppy kids, and nerds. Learning to communicate between all the cultural barriers at that time and being able to blend in with all races and cliques eventually helped me develop a communicative superpower as I grew up. I could talk to any group of people, adapt, and fit in immediately. 🌙

GET HOME SAFE
***

At a social gathering in the City of Angels, the bloody feud between the Bloods and Crips erupted in gunfire. Two young black men were struck, one rushed to the hospital while the other lay on the ground, his life force ebbing away. The raw emotions of his friends made them unable to act in that crucial moment, but my military training kicked in, and I sprang to his aid. I scrambled to find something to staunch the flow of blood, and a kind soul offered me a blanket. I used it to tie a tourniquet around his wound, and we set out to ferry him to the hospital. However, our efforts were thwarted by the very people who are sworn to protect and serve. Suddenly, squad cars screeched onto the scene, ordering us to drag the victim back out of the car and deposit him on the pavement. Law enforcement officials then created a perimeter around him, idly watching as he continued to hemorrhage, a pathetic parody of their sworn duty to protect and serve. He drifted in and out of consciousness, a chilling indictment of public safety gone awry. Ironically, transporting him to the hospital ourselves would have been both quicker and more cost-effective than waiting for the ambulance. But now, in addition to his harrowing injuries, the young man would be saddled with a hefty bill. The crowd grew restless and frustrated, demanding action from the law enforcement officers who had failed to act. This angered one of the cops and a white bald male cop begins to start threatening everyone to back up and gets in one guy's face an inch away and starts screaming at him to back up. His eyes were filled with anger and hate. I was confused because we were yelling at them to help stop the bleeding and instead he was trying to intimidate the crowd, once again, for telling him to help (humanity holding "public safety officials" accountable). The crowd began to get more and more disrespectful when they saw the cops weren't going to help him, and we all became

EXPERIENCE
* * *

enraged (collective consciousness rising). I started communicating with one of the cops to tie a tourniquet on him. The cop was surprised, unbeknownst to him I was a Marine, that I knew the proper procedure to save him. It was at this point, I saw in his eyes, the cop knew that he was in the wrong, and that he could have helped but chose not to. His eyes turned to that of a puppy who just got spanked for eating a shoe. This was one of my first experiences as an adult, living away from home, of a broken system from multiple perspectives. Witnessing willfully ignorant leadership, systemically racist recruiting, white-supremacist-minded employees ensuring the synthetic and artificial medical system got its pennies from the poor, and the desensitized inhumane character of LAPD. This single experience was one of the first times I felt myself begin to awaken to what was really happening in the world, and I knew immediately this was not how humanity was supposed to exist on Earth. The system was broken, but the agent Smiths of the world, comfortable with the crumbs of material possessions they were earning, were the only ones protecting it. Trying to convince the rest of us everything was fine. In the end, the young man that I tied a blanket above his wound, did end up surviving. 🌙

GET HOME SAFE
***

The saying "follow your dreams and you can be anything you want in life" is often told to children, but it's important to have role models who embody this message. I strive to be one of those role models. ☀

Marvel superheroes are just Agent Smiths protecting the matrix. Thanos was Neo. 🌙

Would you value the person who gave you a fishing rod or the person who taught you how to fish? The latter is more valuable as they have taught you a skill that you can use for life. ☀

As you get older, the villains start to make a lot of sense. 🌙

I was asked what triggered the change in my perspective. I was always a leader who stood for what's right, and I wanted to inspire young people from similar backgrounds to find someone who stood by good morals and principles and succeeded in telling our story. It's time to change the glorification of ignorance. ☀

Success is all mental. Your mind may tell you to stop, but if you convince yourself to keep going, you'll find you have more in you. Convince your mind to do great things, and your body, environment, and everything else will follow.

☀

EXPERIENCE
* * *

As a leader of over 100 Marines, I learned the best leaders lead from the front. They get down and dirty building the trenches with the lower ranks. That way you build respect amongst your followers. Once you have their respect, and you give an order, they will do it happily at a fast speed. If you come in barking orders, ruling with fear and without earning any respect, they will do it slowly and half-assed. Get your hands dirty, earn respect, and eventually you can sit back in an office and give orders without ever getting your hands dirty again. 🌙

I will always communicate openly and transparently with others. Despite the challenges that life presents, I aim to provide guidance, wisdom, and knowledge to help others overcome them and reach their full potential. ☀

GET HOME SAFE

***

Keep it simple. This guidebook is a collection of thoughts gathered from books, personal experiences, wisdom from mentors, and interviews with childhood heroes. It's up to you to decide what to do with the information. These are the things that have propelled me forward. ☀

Every human should go through an individuation process of being alone. A lonesome journey of self-evaluation to find and feel where your soul and purpose aligns. After they are done, they should be welcomed back into a community, a tribe, or a village operating as a collective state of consciousness. This is how humanity is supposed to exist. 🌙

Formerly, I thought that owning fancy cars, having a lot of wealth, leading a gang, and having multiple relationships was a sign of power. However, I now know that I was misguided and not well-informed. Real power lies in creating wealth for future generations, guiding my family through tough times, and changing the fate of my community for years to come. Material possessions hold less value than intangible things. ☀

EXPERIENCE
***

A collective state of consciousness is when the people living together make decisions that benefit the entire community and not just themselves. 🌙

I am an introvert by nature and enjoy solitude, but when I discovered my purpose, I felt that creating the Teach Peace NYC clothing line was the best way to spread my messages. Although the profits will eventually fade and the clothes will deteriorate over time, I felt that selling mostly through e-commerce limited my interactions with others. That's why I started writing and hosting a podcast. The impact that I have on others through my audio, literature, and interactions is timeless and will last forever, so I stepped out of my comfort zone. ☀

I would not be proud if my daughter brought home a past version of me. I did not know how to treat a woman until I had my daughter. I didn't know how to protect, provide, and produce for the women in my life until I was about 25-26. It was the generational curse of having no masculine guidance that instilled this negative attribute in my life. 🌙

GET HOME SAFE
✼ ✼ ✼

One lasting memory has had a profound effect on my perspective on life. When I was under ten years old, I overheard my mother crying on the phone to a friend during the holidays, saying she wouldn't be able to fulfill our Christmas wish list. Despite the fact that we did receive gifts, that conversation has stayed with me, and I promised myself that as long as I had the energy, I would make sure my family never suffered again. ☀

Artificial intelligence can be used for an immense amount of good, but the opposite is true as well. If you have a good heart and care about humanity, learn to code so you can protect others who will use technology for evil purposes. 🌙

I candidly discuss my struggles with depression, including the loss of my mother who was my biggest supporter. It's normal to have periods of sadness and low productivity, but it's important to recognize and push through these times for the benefit of ourselves and others. I hope my experiences and wisdom can offer comfort and encouragement to others. ☀

EXPERIENCE
***

I talk to myself out loud so I can get guidance from my ancestors. 🌙

I draw on my personal experiences to offer guidance. I used to prioritize work, socializing, and impressing others, but it's never too late to change. I believe in your ability to change too. ☀️

The public education system prepares you to become a mentally submissive employee to the economic system, aka the matrix. They do not want you to have the ability to critically think on your own and have a solution based mindset. It's easier for the people in power to control an ignorantly obedient populace than an intellectually creative populace. The school system is similar to a prison system. They want you to have fixed responses to authority, enforce a huge emphasis on silence and order, have children walk in lines, negative reinforcement when a child misbehaves, lose your individual autonomy to critically think and be creative on your own, you have no input on any decisions, and have set times for walking and eating. 🌙

GET HOME SAFE
* * *

Embrace challenges and use them to grow stronger. Despite losing my mother at 18, not knowing my father, and struggling with depression, I was able to turn my pain into passion. I became the manager of three top medical research companies without a degree and wrote this guidebook to help others navigate life's challenges. The hardships I faced have made me the person I am today, and I wouldn't change a thing about my story except losing my mother. Change your mindset and be prepared for anything life may bring. ☀

The American public education system may be the worst education system ever known to man. Aquire books and create your own library of information that interests you. Use your phone as a tool and teach yourself. Become friends with people who are where you want to be and be humble enough to shut your mouth and learn from them. 🌙

I approach this from a personal perspective, not with a sense of superiority. I have experienced depression, financial difficulties and lived in poverty for much of my life. My aim is to impart lessons learned from my struggles to others facing similar challenges. I've shared my story and philosophy with friends in hallways, and now I have the opportunity to share it with a wider audience. I hope my experiences can bring peace, mindfulness, and serenity to others, just as it has for me. ☀

EXPERIENCE
***

The majority of doctors aren't healers or nurturers, they're just pharmaceutical distributors. Bring back the shamans. 🌙

Society has often labeled me with negative stereotypes such as criminal, gang member, and project kid, without knowing who I truly am. Remember that someone else's opinion of you is not important. ☀

I still haven't found camaraderie and a bond amongst men like I did in the Marine Corps. Most men would solve their mental health issues if they found a pack of like-minded men who motivated and pushed one another to their prime masculine limits like a pride of lions or a pack of wolves. The majority of men have a group of friends who feed into their vices, addictions, and weaknesses with no accountability. 🌙

GET HOME SAFE
***

People often tell me to slow down and take a break, but then later ask for help or want to know my secrets for success. Don't let these outside voices affect you. Focus on your goals and don't let anyone else's opinions distract you. Work hard now so that you can relax later. ☀

Current war of the matrix is the spiritually elite verse the economically elite. 🌙

Since my teenage years, I've worked various jobs and pursued side businesses just to bring home a few dollars to tell my mom she didn't have to cook dinner. However, since my mother's passing, money has lost its appeal and only covers bills and buys things that lose value. The love and feedback I receive from my community when I create keeps me going, even though not everyone will understand. ☀

EXPERIENCE
***

Moments of hostility between intelligence and ignorance, ignorance is normally the first to attack. 🌙

Sharing both my successes and struggles, one challenge I struggle with is becoming too attached to those I try to help. I've realized growth cannot be forced and I need to focus my efforts on those who are with me on this journey, providing information and experiences through my books, social media, and podcast. Appreciate those who are with you and keep moving forward, the rope will be there for others when they are ready. ☀

That self-made mentality really is disrespectful to everyone who helped you out along the way. 🌙

I am grateful for the good. I am grateful for the bad. Thank God I learn from both. ☀

GET HOME SAFE
***

Isolation raises your frequency. 🌙

Merely another flawed human, striving to rise above adversity. ☀

When women respond to negative comments about themselves by reacting impulsively with violence, they undermine their own beauty. 🌙

Authentic leaders must embrace their failures, harness the lessons learned to drive themselves forward, and have the fortitude to try again and make the next challenging decision ☀

EXPERIENCE
✳✳✳

If you're a man who is depressed or low on energy, here's the remedy to restore your natural energy back to full strength. Go 72 days without ejaculating. That's your life force you're continuously depleting. You charge your phone but don't charge your body? The more you ejaculate, the quicker you age. If you're in your late 20's or early 30's with grey hair, that means you're malnourished. Most of your minerals are stored in your testicles. So, when you over ejaculate and deplete your body of these minerals, your body begins to pull minerals from your skin, bones, and hair. Semen retention needs to be a cultural tradition in order to bring back strong, wise, and disciplined men. 🌙

I hustle, I pray, and I'll do it all again tomorrow ☀

Humans are natural sun migrators. We were not meant to sign a lease and live in one location for years on end. 🌙

Every day I ask the heavens to keep me safe. I'll handle the rest. ☀

GET HOME SAFE
✶ ✶ ✶

Whoever said, "Only God can judge me", didn't want to be held accountable for their actions. Humans are always judging one another. We have to in order to assess people before we allow them into our personal space. We judge each other based on principles, ideologies, codes of conduct, and familiarity. Being a vegan is a food principle. Saving or investing money from every check is a financial principle. Having the sexual discipline to not sleep with any and every person you find attractive is a self-discipline principle. We are always judging one another and I will personally judge any and everyone before I allow them into the company of not only myself, but especially if they are to come into the company of my children. 🌙

I don't want my family to face the same struggles I faced when I was born. I consider that a failure. I want my children to surpass my achievements much faster. That's why I can't just give them the same blueprint and hope for a miracle. I need to change the NARRATIVE, starting with myself. ☀

That whole street mentality of being real and fake, we need to kill that shit. You've got to evolve. When you evolve, you're constantly changing your characteristics and what you stand for when new information presents itself. The more experiences you have, the more you learn, the more you open your mind. We are always going to change. That whole, "You're being fake, you're being different" is them still stuck at the same level of consciousness. Fuck that shit. Be different. They are going to perceive it and project it as being fake because you aren't the same person they first met. And that's okay. 🌙

EXPERIENCE
***

Beware, for snakes often come disguised with friendly handshakes and smiling faces ☀

As a leader and healer, you can't save everybody. If you try to save everybody, you're going to drain yourself. Have the awareness to evaluate if the person you're trying to help has the intention to self-develop. If not, keep the conversation topics simple, like news, sports, and the weather. If the person is ready to self-develop, you don't want to push them over the edge. You may just want to pat them on the back and ease them into the process. The smallest accomplishments that you achieved when you were in your teens or twenties may be huge for someone just starting to self-develop in their 30s. You don't want to belittle their accomplishments by gloating about your own. Be patient with your Padawans. 🌙

As a leader, whether in a corporate or athletic setting, you are not superior to others, but rather have assumed a greater responsibility. It is your obligation to cultivate the best in each individual, foster trust, and consistently bring forth the best version of yourself as a model for others to emulate. ☀

GET HOME SAFE
✱ ✱ ✱

You're a high vibrational entity existing in a physical vessel. Your body is a biological antenna, your mind is the electricity, and your soul is the frequency it resonates at. In laymen's terms, your body is a car, your mind is the driver, and your soul is the radio station. You may be operating at a frequency of 101.1 and your significant other may be a 93.7. You may need to find someone operating at a 102.3 who better understands how to reciprocate your energy. 🌙

There's a shortage of genuine energy and principles in the world today. ☀

The military taught me that humans flourish in a village. It took me awhile to realize why it was so hard to transition back to civilian life. American society has destroyed the village and promotes individualism. Being independent may be one of the most self-sabotaging, egotistical characteristics pushed onto the minds of Americans. 🌙

EXPERIENCE
***

One of my biggest regrets as an adult is not investing in myself earlier, when I started earning my own money after high school. Instead, I spent my money on expensive clothes and accessories for temporary social status. Investing in your message, your impact on others, and your legacy is much more important than any materialistic items. I strongly encourage you to invest in yourself and your message. ☀

Those who do the bare minimum and have low standards of themselves will die trying to convince you that at least they are doing something. Doing something is only one step ahead of doing nothing. 🌙

The current iteration of myself wasn't constructed in a day. It's a combination of experience, growth, and a daily journey through pain, struggle, survival, and sacrifice. ☀

GET HOME SAFE
***

In today's day and age, there are three parents. Mom, Dad, and the iPad. 🌙

American society is missing a key component for humanity's sanity— the village. Bringing back the village would help a lot of people's mental health issues and day-to-day stresses imposed by the pressure of surviving independently in this society. 🌙

I matured from pain not age. "They" won't understand. ☀️

For the sake of the healthy development of your children, individuals have to stop being bitter when their child's mother or father after a significant time of being separated, finds a new partner. If you learn to communicate without hostility and build a bond for the benefit of the child, you now have an additional source of support to help you with your child. A lot of you self-sabotage yourselves into single motherhood or fatherhood because you were incapable of being emotionally mature enough to dissolve your bitterness and jealousy. 🌙

EXPERIENCE
✳ ✳ ✳

How I handle negative events in life determines my character and the quality of my existence. I can choose to dwell in sadness, unable to move on from my loss, or I can choose to overcome the pain and appreciate the most valuable gift I possess, which is life itself. ☀

Most people exist in the ego state of consciousness, which has them hyper focused on themselves. They have not elevated enough to be able to practice duality. Duality is when they transfer the frequency and perspective of their consciousness from their ego (self-love) to their soul (selfless-love) so they can connect with those around them. It makes it hard for them to relate to others outside of their own situation. 🌙

When you come from difficult circumstances, you hope to move past survival and live life to the fullest. Everyone should know that the world is bigger than their city, and just because no one who looks like you have done what you want to do, doesn't mean it's impossible. Stay consistent, manifest your goals, be genuine and kind, and good things will happen. ☀

GET HOME SAFE
***

Some people will perceive you as the issue, so they don't have to elevate out of their comfort zone. 🌙

Wake up every day with gratitude for the roof over your head and being blessed. Life's minor obstacles can easily be forgotten when we remember the bigger picture. My experiences at Weil Cornell Medicine and Memorial Sloan Kettering taught me the importance of perspective. A visit to the pediatric cancer center, where I saw kids from all over the world fighting for their lives and emotionally drained parents, gave me a new appreciation for what's truly important. So, let's start each day with gratitude and realize just how blessed we truly are. Peace ya. ☀

Unfortunately, the truth will never travel as fast as a lie. 🌙

EXPERIENCE

***

Shortcuts to knowledge may come with some fine print. 🌙

I hold the belief that life itself is a form of art, including the way you express your thoughts, the manner in which you conduct yourself, the way you love others, your beliefs and aspirations, the decoration of your home, the food you prepare, and your emotions. All these elements together create a masterpiece that is life. ☀

If your desire is to be rich, you will become connected to wealth and less connected to your soul from the desire of greed. If your desire is to be enlightened, you will become connected to health, your natural soul, but disconnected from wealth in order to detach from material possessions. You'll need to find a balance of both if you wish to flourish in the belly of the beast called the American Economy. (Ego/Economy) vs.(Soul/Ecology)

GET HOME SAFE
***

The four key elements that have driven my growth are Confidence, Courage, Creativity, and Consistency. • Confidence means having faith in yourself and your abilities and speaking your goals into existence. • Courage enables you to face challenges and step outside your comfort zone, knowing that even if you lose, you can always win again. • Creativity involves consistently finding new ways to express yourself, with authenticity and in line with your core values. • And ultimately, Consistency is the most crucial of all, as it's what makes the other C's matter. ☀

Kratos, from the God of War video game, taught me a lot on how to be a father to a son. 🌙

We are spiritual beings experiencing a human existence, not human beings having a spiritual experience. ☀

Embrace every day of your life without regret. The happy days bring joy, the challenging days offer valuable lessons, and the best days become cherished memories. ☀

EXPERIENCE
✳ ✳ ✳

Everything came from a thought. Whether it was a selfish or selfless thought is to be determined by the creator and the observer of the thought. This is where disagreements begin. 🌙

Never be afraid to share your story, including the struggles and the people who helped you overcome them. Your story can be an inspiration to others. ☀

Depression can tip toe in like a vampire in the shadows. Your healthy habits and day-to-day consistency is what continues to ignite the flame of light that burns in your soul. Stay disciplined and that vampire will never be able to step out of the shadows and into your light. 🌙

GET HOME SAFE
***

Rest, because the matrix will burn you out and keep moving forward over your dead body without a second thought. Be wary tho because too much rest can turn into comfortable complacency. 🌙

Great leaders achieve success by working closely with their team, leading with purpose, building relationships, seeking input, and standing side by side with their team. Strengthen those relationships to ensure everyone is on the same page and working towards a shared vision. ☀

The best leaders prioritize their team's needs over their own and earn their trust by following through on their commitments. They build relationships to better serve their team and lead from the front lines. ☀

Once you speak, you're judged. Thinking before you speak, that's wisdom. 🌙

EXPERIENCE
***

There is no success without stress. 🌙

To the youth: Losing my mother taught me the importance of cherishing life's precious moments. Appreciate your mothers and grandmothers, as one day you may not have them. Instead of buying expensive sneakers, do something special for your mom, like treating her to a spa day or just giving her a hug and telling her you love her. ☀

Witnessing so much ignorance in my culture and community was one of the defining moments I chose to write this book. I realized through my investments in real estate that it didn't matter how much someone fixed the community. The lack of intelligence in the community would destroy it no matter how beautiful you rebuilt it. So, I decided to start with the basics and focus on repairing the mindset. No political point of views or religious debates, only quick lessons and life principles that upload immediately into the mind (Physical) and soul (Spiritual) to enrich the electromagnetic energy of one's aura. 🌙

GET HOME SAFE
***

Your diet is not only what you eat but also what you listen to. 🌙

Just because someone wronged me, it doesn't mean I will talk badly about them. Even when it hurts, one must remain steadfast. ☀

I too experience depression, anxiety, and overwhelm at times, but I keep pushing forward, even if it's just taking one small step on my toughest days. Sometimes, going through the worst leads to the best. ☀

A person's eyes will speak louder than their words. 🌙

EXPERIENCE
***

People speak of the light and dark as different personalities. They assume light is good and dark is bad which is not true. Too much light makes you foolish, and too much dark makes you selfish. The light is about being selfless, operating at a collective state of consciousness— the soul. Putting the goals of the community before personal desire. You care about others, but too much love can allow selfish people to take advantage of your kindness and leech off your energy. The dark is about being selfish, operating at an independent state of consciousness— the ego. You care about yourself— self-love— and this can be healthy form of preserving your energy and thoughts from outside sources, but too much darkness will make you a predator. You're willing to sabotage anyone else's happiness for your own personal benefit. You need the yin and the yang to balance one another out. 🌙

Don't judge others based on their appearance. No one knows the struggles they went through to get where they are. ☀

Growing requires letting go of our past thoughts and beliefs. After losing my mother, I had a choice to make. I could either let my heartache consume me or channel that energy into doing good for others. I hope to see her proud of me when I reach the gates. ☀

GET HOME SAFE
***

It's not failure we fear, but the perception of failure by others, that blocks the path to our blessings and potential.

☀

Leaving your hometown is crucial for personal growth and avoiding mental stagnation in a comfortable environment. Remaining in your birthplace establishes a routine that breeds complacency. However, this comfort can render you stagnant in various aspects of life—mentally, physically, emotionally, and spiritually. It leads to repetitiveness.

Without venturing beyond your comfort zone on a journey of self-development, you miss out on the chance to encounter new and challenging situations that foster intellectual and skill advancement. For instance, you won't have the opportunity to engage with diverse cultures, adopt a problem-solving mindset, connect with inspiring mentors and like-minded communities that hold you to higher standards, or broaden your perspective through exposure to different geographic locations.

If you don't expose yourself to alternative ways of life and thinking beyond your current social circle, it's time to seek out a new one. This aligns with the saying, "Show me your friends, and I'll show you your future." Your mindset is heavily influenced by your surroundings and the people you interact with daily. If you do step out your comfort zone and leave your hometown you will realize most of the individuals you know who may physically be 45 years old, but mentally, they are still have the mindset of an 18-year-old. 🌙

EXPERIENCE
* * *

Take note of the times of disappointment, challenge, and uncertainty because, upon reaching your goals, you can use those experiences to help others who are feeling the same. ☀

With how much you post on social media, the government doesn't need to spy on you. You spy on yourself every time you post. So, if you don't respect the privacy of your own life, don't get mad when people speak on it. 🌙

The lesson I learned from a close friend's sentence is that one should avoid glorifying criminal activities on social media. The praise and followers are insignificant compared to the consequences of losing freedom, family support, and the ability to spend holidays with loved ones. Instead, we should make wisdom, intelligence, accountability, and caring for family the true glory. Supporting your family is the real definition of "gangsta".

GET HOME SAFE
* * *

I cannot provide a specific script or blueprint for my success. Instead, I focused on showing up daily, treating people with respect, seeking wisdom, and having good intentions. The blessings followed as a result. ☀

There are two types of people: people who are okay with hearing comfortable lies, and people who would rather hear uncomfortable truths. 🌙

I can guide you through my path to success, but your journey will be unique to you. The lessons you take from experiences may differ from mine, but I aim to show you that it is possible. Only you can pursue your own dream, as each person's purpose is custom-made.

EXPERIENCE
***

I don't judge people based on their habits, job, appearance, or decisions. Everyone doesn't have the same access to knowledge, experience, or opportunities as others. Appearances can be deceiving, and one's job or situation in life doesn't define who they are. You always have the chance to grow and improve until you physically pass away. ☀

As I'm writing this book, I'm assessing learning points at different stages of my life. I've recently learnt that it's important for a parent to acknowledge their child's accomplishments at pivotal points. Don't use the phrase, "I'm proud of you.", too frequently. Use it when they've accomplished and conquered an intense life obstacle. If you say you are proud of them all the time, you will dilute the meaning and value of the phrase. Eventually your child's standards will become comfortable at that level of acceptance. They will lose their drive to show and prove themselves, in time, becoming content. I've learnt to be selective when I say it. 🌙

I strive to pass down my wisdom, experiences, and knowledge to future generations. I am no longer interested in material possessions that lose value over time. I strive to make every dollar count. ☀

GET HOME SAFE
***

Everyone wants to be the boss. Until they see the day-to-day responsibilities of a boss. Who doesn't have the luxury to make excuses for things not getting done. 🌙

Learn from your mistakes. Despite not graduating from college, struggling in high school, quitting football, and facing depression, I am now able to write a book to inspire others. Embrace both the good and bad times in life, use these experiences to grow and help others. ☀

Feeling down? Use the natural elements of nature to recharge your soul. 1.) Ground your feet or meditate on the EARTH to gather negative electrons. 2.) Do a cold WATER plunge and drink free flowing water. 3.) Make time for FIREside journaling while doing most of your thinking staring into the FIRE. 4.) Take very long extended breaths of forest or beach AIR, in and out, to relax the muscles and brain waves (Thoughts). 5.) SUN gaze at sunrise and sunset to charge your neurons. 6.) Find a green space and FOREST bathe absorbing the naturally energized negative electrons in the air. 🌙

EXPERIENCE
***

I recall a time in 2012 when I had no clear direction in life. My friends were pursuing careers as EMTs, so I invested time and money in a three-month course. I passed the course with the highest grade but failed the state test twice. I felt defeated as I watched my peers advance in their careers. However, one month into the second course, I received an entry-level position in medical research. Ten years later, I have successfully managed three major research companies and have held my own in meetings with top scientists, veterinarians, and doctors. Consistency always prevails in the end, and the universe will eventually reward your hard work.

Everything happens for a reason. ☀

The main mission of our soul's existence, from the moment of birth, is how we elevate through life when we are faced with problems and obstacles. Using our creativity to come up with solutions while maintaining a calm state of mind when the issue arises will determine whether our life ascends into bliss or descends into chaotic suffering. 🌙

I have held leadership positions where I have helped others grow and improve. Despite any rewards or recognition, my true joy came from seeing others reach new heights due to my positive influence. Inspiring others is the greatest act one can achieve. ☀

GET HOME SAFE
✳ ✳ ✳

Emotional difficulties, such as betrayal, disappointment, anger, heartbreak, and pain, are a part of life. During these times, your energy may be drained, and you may consider giving up. You may question why you should continue in a world that thrives on negativity. Despite these challenges, I am grateful for my experiences and would not change a thing. I sleep soundly with a clear conscience knowing that I am making a positive change in the world. ☀

Don't wait until you're retired and about to die to make a bucket list. Make one now. Research the first one on your list. Come up with a plan of action. How much will travel cost? How many hours do I have to work, or items do I have to sell, or services do I have to provide to make this happen? Accomplish that goal little by little, day by day, and then go fucking do it. Experience life now, while you're young, not when death is knocking at your door. Ask yourself, how easier would it be to experience those things if you had friends putting their money together for the same goal? 🌙

My aim is not to prove myself superior, but to inspire and bring out the best in others. I hope that I can show that success can be achieved with a pure heart and integrity. Instead of trying to prove someone else's intellectual inferiority, I hope to attract those who align with my values and join me on this journey. Everyone deserves to be unique and respected. ☀

EXPERIENCE
***

If someone continuously drains your soul on a day-to-day basis it's time to remove them from your day to day existence. 🌙

To become my best self, I had to eliminate old habits and ego. I sought guidance from mentors and asked tough questions about myself and the world. This led me to discover untapped potential and a deeper understanding of the world beyond my familiar surroundings. ☀

I experienced a beautiful childhood. I am grateful for my mother for all that she sacrificed to make that happen. 🌙

Lead with a clear purpose, build trust with your team by treating everyone equally, and strive to have a positive impact on others. Kind leadership is a strength, not a weakness, as long as it is not taken advantage of. ☀

GET HOME SAFE
***

Did you have a good childhood? If you did, then go look who ever raised you, in the eyes, and tell them thank you. If you didn't, ensure you don't pass down your childhood trauma and generational curses on to your children. 🌙

The best revenge against those who betray, manipulate, or use you is to become the best version of yourself. Focus on your personal growth, elevating your energy, and sharing positivity with others. The universe will reciprocate the energy you put out. Don't waste time on negativity. Pursue love, peace, and happiness. ☀

Not all opportunities are measured in dollars. ☀

After growing up in small poverty-stricken town in America I'll never forget the first time I laid eyes on southern California. It was my first time living on my own. I felt like I landed in heaven, and couldn't wait to explore. The experience of traveling broadened my mind to incomprehensible levels. 🌙

EXPERIENCE
***

For a period of time in my mid-twenties, after I got out of the military, I was lost. Unsure of who I was now that I no longer had the honored status of wearing the United States Marine Corps uniform. I was no longer Sergeant Rodriguez. I was back to being Christopher Rodriguez and wasn't sure who that guy was or was going to become. I remember who I was in High School and knew I couldn't take care of my family operating in that immature mindset. I remembered who I was in the Marine Corps, but no longer carried the title of my rank or the respect that came with it. I had no idea what was next. So, I went into self-isolation for a couple years and I read... A lot. 🌙

Your healing, progress, or journey is unique to you and not dependent on anyone else's timeline. Your growth is also not impacted by external factors. Don't rush the process to meet others' expectations, instead focus on being present and enjoying the journey. ☀

GET HOME SAFE
***

The military was a beautiful village of men and women who worked together as a collective state of consciousness. Unfortunately, there were a lot of men and women who took advantage of their rank and made people's lives miserable for their own personal satisfaction. Seeing people being treated unfairly activated this burning sensation of anger in my chest. I would have to release this internal uproar vocally or else my soul would feel like it was going to explode. Many higher ranking members didn't like this quality about me. Countless times I stood up for lower ranking Marines against higher ranking Marines. This allowed me to acquire an immense amount of respect from the lower ranks to the point the higher ranks could no longer control anyone I was in charge of. Never underestimate the power of your voice. You may be standing alone when you first speak but by the time you're done you may have a hundred people standing behind who felt the same way. They were just too scared to be the first one to speak up. 🌙

EXPERIENCE

***

Today's culture and society often perpetuate violence, hate, and negativity. Protect your heart and mind every day and don't be afraid to stand alone in spreading love.

The world desperately needs someone like you. ☀

When I wore a suit in public for no particular reason, people assumed I was a wealthy business owner. However, when I wore a black hoodie with a bandana over my head, people kept their distance. Similarly, wearing sweatpants and flip-flops every day made me feel increasingly lazy. Conversely, wearing workout attire motivated me to exercise. Your clothing not only affects people's initial perceptions of you, but also influences your own self-perception, which can affect your behavior throughout the day. It's important to be mindful of how you dress because looking good often translates to feeling good, and feeling good can lead to greater productivity and success. 🌙

Most of us desire to feel loved, appreciated, and noticed. Take the time to recognize and show appreciation to those around you, whether it be someone close to you, someone on social media, or even yourself. Let them know their efforts matter. ☀

Fix your issues today so you can wake up to new issues tomorrow. Progress is a process. 🌙

GET HOME SAFE
***

Many unfortunate scenarios could have been avoided if I had been more emotionally aware and refrained from impulsively reacting based on my initial rush of emotions. Instead, I should have taken a step back, relaxed, and tactfully assessed the situation in order to formulate a well-thought-out response or plan. To behave and conduct ourselves respectfully, we must learn to reassess how we respond to adversity. 🌙

I cannot provide a specific script or blueprint for my success. Instead, I focused on showing up daily, treating people with respect, seeking wisdom, and having good intentions. The blessings followed as a result. ☀

Whenever a problem arises, I tend to draw on similar experiences from my past to find a solution. However, there is one crucial factor to consider when attempting to resolve a new problem: whether there were any negative consequences resulting from my previous solution. It's essential to evaluate whether the previous solution had an immediate positive impact but negative consequences in the long run or vice versa. The key takeaway is that we must teach ourselves to unlearn and relearn how we respond to various issues. 🌙

My Dearest Self, I am overwhelmingly proud of the individual you have evolved into from your past trials and tribulations. Certain moments of struggle felt they would never end. You persisted in your growth, and you shall soon be compensated for your unwavering dedication to spreading love, peace, and uplifting those around you. Never, ever, stop. ☀

EXPERIENCE
***

Your past experiences are the training you needed to conquer your current circumstances. 🌙

Being alone is terrifyingly beautiful. ☀

MINDSET
✴✴✴

The 6 W's of a Man or Woman of Excellence
-Well Read
-Well Dressed
-Well Behaved
-Well Spoken
-Well Traveled
-Well Trained 🌙

Embrace the challenges that serve to educate, steer, and foster growth, allowing you to generate and safeguard your energy. Trials and turbulence serve a purpose in life, imparting understanding and enabling one to pass on the valuable lessons learned, inspiring others along the way. ☀

We all need the 3 B's. Balance, breaks, and boundaries. 🌙

GET HOME SAFE
* * *

4 Factors Every Successful Man or Woman Should Self-audit

1.) Sociological Health - Environment & People
2.) Biological Health - Body, Diet, Gut, Brain, Circadian Rhythm, Exercises, Vitamins & Minerals
3.) Psychological Health - Mindfulness, Reading Habits, Education Credits, Coachability, Unhealed Traumas, Positive Self Image, Creativity, Beliefs, Cognitive Bias
4.) Spiritual Health - Know Your Shadow Self, Purpose Driven Work, Sense of Well-Being, Karma, Good Deeds, Holistic Health, Interconnected, Alignment, Deep Connections, Meditation Schedule, Time in Nature. 🌙

Performing a self-audit is an essential practice for personal and professional growth. It involves taking an honest look at oneself to identify strengths, weaknesses, and areas for improvement. By regularly conducting self-audits, individuals can gain a deeper understanding of themselves, their behaviors, and their impact on others, and make necessary changes to achieve their goals. 🌙

MINDSET
✶✶✶

2 Types of Minds

When faced with a problem, a mature mind approaches the situation with composure and level-headedness. This type of mind utilizes its higher reasoning skills to process the available information and come up with a solution-based outcome. On the other hand, an immature mind tends to react impulsively and allow its emotions to take over. This often leads to feeling overwhelmed and complaining about the problem rather than actively seeking a solution.

It's important to cultivate a mature mind in order to effectively navigate life's challenges and make progress towards our goals. This involves developing skills such as emotional regulation, critical thinking, and problem-solving. 🌙

Holding oneself accountable is often the most challenging task. We are quick to hold others accountable, but we let ourselves fall into patterns of repeated mistakes. Making mistakes is natural, but it's our responsibility to acknowledge and correct them if they don't align with our long-term goals. ☀

If you think discipline is hard, imagine living without it. ☀

Prepare for adversity while hoping for peace. ☀

GET HOME SAFE
***

2 Levels of Observers
-A low level observer is controlled by what they see.
-A high level observer controls what they see. 🌙

Never take away someone's hope as it might be all they have left. ☀

4 E's of Growth
-Execution
-Experience
-Education
-Environment 🌙

Enlightenment signifies not only the cessation of suffering and internal conflict, but also the liberation from the constant bondage of incessant thought. ☀

MINDSET
***

Clarity is key to creating your best work. Though discipline and hard work are important, taking breaks and prioritizing self-care are crucial for maintaining energy and finding solutions to problems. Some of the best work comes from taking a rest day, waking up early and taking time for yourself. Be kind to yourself so you can be great for others. ☀

Order on the outside does wonders to tame the chaos on the inside. 🌙

I avoid comparisons with others. Each person has their own unique experiences, challenges, upbringing, beliefs, support systems, values, and background. Every journey is different, and someone else's success does not diminish my worth or increase it because of their failures. It's easy to focus on one's weaknesses compared to others' strengths and neglect our own worth. Comparison is often said to steal happiness and I firmly believe that my own value and energy will bring me everything that I am meant to have in life. It's a competition between myself and myself only. ☀

GET HOME SAFE
***

You're an enemy to yourself when you give everyone else your time. 🌙

Stoicism- the endurance of pain or hardship without the display of feelings and without complaint. ☀

Saying "no" is crucial, because saying "yes" is costly. 🌙

Your thoughts and actions shape your reality, so cultivate a positive mindset and believe in your ability to succeed. Speak your aspirations into existence and enjoy the journey. ☀

MINDSET
✱ ✱ ✱

A man who has a dangerous past but is striving to be a better person can ultimately benefit humanity more than a good man who lacks the capacity for danger. The latter may never develop the courage to stand up against evil and may instead choose to turn a blind eye, effectively becoming a silent accomplice to the wrongdoing around him. 🌙

History holds valuable knowledge. Don't reinvent the wheel, learn from the mistakes of successful people in various fields. Seek out the wisdom that elevated them to greatness and apply these lessons to your own journey.
The answers have already been found. ☀

Bad men are necessary for humanity. They keep the evil men away from the door of the innocent. 🌙

GET HOME SAFE
***

To manifest effectively, you must be confident and have a clear vision of your goal. Visualize reaching the finish line and eliminate any doubts that may hinder the manifestation process. ☀

In times of chaos, panic does nothing. Harness it. Let it serve you. 🌙

Guard your energy by being mindful of the things you invest your time and energy in. Avoid topics or discussions that don't align with your mission and prioritize your energy towards things that matter. ☀

MINDSET
***

A young man's judgement is clouded when he is too eager to prove himself as a man. 🌙

Life is not always going to be easy but stay disciplined and focused on your goals despite the circumstances. ☀

There are unsung heroes among us who may never receive the recognition they deserve, while the most popular celebrities are often individuals who perform an act in the public eye. Regardless, strive to exhibit kindness and compassion towards others, without concern for receiving acknowledgment or praise. 🌙

Success is not a pursuit, but rather an outcome drawn to you by the person you choose to become. ☀

Approach others with kindness, understanding that they may be facing their own challenges. ☀

You deserve the best in every aspect - happiness, compassion, love, finances, and empathy. ☀

GET HOME SAFE
***

Try to be of service to others whenever possible. You may be the only one to show them love. If you see someone being ignored, include them. If you see someone being silenced, listen to them. If you see someone being brought down, lift them up. Stand for something, or the cycle will continue. ☀

A king, or queen, may only consider another king a friend, everyone else will either follow or oppose their leadership. 🌙

Don't get too caught up in the future, cherish and make the most of each moment in the present. ☀

MINDSET
***

Pain is part of the process. If you avoid pain, you're going to fuck up the progress. 🌙

Your mindset has the power to transform your life, focus on becoming the person you want to be to attract success.

Another person's excellence doesn't decrease your own. Only your perception of self will allow that to happen.

🌙

GET HOME SAFE
***

Take responsibility for your life and success, eliminate the victim mentality and make intentional choices to reach your goals. ☀

If your mind is blind to the possibility, then your eyes will be blind to the opportunity. 🌙

Healing is a difficult journey that requires change in your thinking, speech, relationships, and what you allow into your life. You must take control of your story and not let your past dictate your future. Acknowledge your experiences, live in the present, and keep moving forward. ☀

MINDSET
***

You can't change your life if you don't change your habits. 🌙

The internet and social media give everyone a platform to be heard. Don't be discouraged by negativity or hate comments. Stay true to your values and principles, don't waste time arguing with others. ☀

Emotions trigger thoughts. Thoughts are like clouds. If you attach an emotion to a cloud, it can create a beautiful sunny day or a category five hurricane. 🌙

GET HOME SAFE
***

Start each day by affirming your greatness and expressing gratitude for the blessings in your life. Own both the positive and negative aspects of your life but begin each day with positive energy and intentions. My only daily request is for safety, and I am confident in my ability to handle everything else. Believing in someone is worth more than gold, support isn't just about finances.

Thoughts are like clouds, sometimes just let them float by. 🌙

To reach new heights, you must shed the things that no longer serve you - people, places, and energies that do not align with your growth. ☀

MINDSET
* * *

A man without a plan will become broken under the pressures of society. He will fail his family and future generations by passing his generational trauma on to his children. 🌙

Self-love and respect cannot be determined by likes or comments, stay true to yourself and your real-life connections. ☀

Masculine competition is encouragingly healthy and necessary for a man's mental health. 🌙

Wisdom is more valuable than silver and gold. ☀

GET HOME SAFE
***

As men, we have an inherent desire to tap into the warrior spirit encoded in our genes. We may choose to develop our fighting skills, acquire property and assets, or even engage in competitive video games to satisfy this primal instinct. The rush of victory and the feeling of conquest are essential to our sense of masculinity, and we feel compelled to demonstrate our strength and defend what is valuable to us. It is akin to the thrill of facing a bear in the woods with nothing but a knife and emerging victorious, standing triumphantly with one foot atop the defeated beast, affirming our worth as men. 🌙

Unlearn and relearn how you respond to disrespect. 🌙

MINDSET
* * *

We all have unique gifts or talents. Don't let traditional education, external influences, or other mental obstructions limit your potential to make a positive impact. Embrace your uniqueness and contribute to the betterment of humanity. ☀

Your morning routine will make or break the productivity of your day. 🌙

I approach everything with sincerity and love, driven by inspiration and good intentions. Despite present challenges, I remain confident in the success of my pursuits. ☀

GET HOME SAFE
***

Unorganized men will become depressed insomniacs from the stress of not accomplishing their desired thoughts of the day. 🌙

The key to a successful business lies in understanding and respecting human aspirations, fostering love and happiness, and creating a sense of fulfillment. Business should aim to serve a higher purpose and enhance one's life journey. ☀

We must learn to release the disappointment and self-inflicted failure of the day, so it doesn't keep us awake at night. 🌙

MINDSET
***

If others doubt you, ignore them and let your hard work do the talking. Instead of getting angry, focus on the people who believe in you and be grateful for their support. ☀

Learn to heal without venting to everyone your pain. 🌙

Work harder and smarter, as inactivity and overthinking can arise when you have too much time on your hands. Take a break and refocus, then apologize for your absence later. ☀

Live in peace but be prepared for war. 🌙

GET HOME SAFE
***

To break free from the mundane 9-5 routine of small-town America, it can be beneficial to venture out and explore new places, broaden your perspectives, and enrich your mind through travel. 🌙

My thoughts, actions, and energy are now centered on inspiration and fueled by love and purity. Without this mindset, progress will be limited. My priorities go deeper than just making money. ☀︎

Being at peace when someone is trying to trigger and antagonize you is a top tier flex. 🌙

MINDSET
***

Holding others accountable is easy, but true growth comes from holding ourselves accountable and staying focused, respecting our time and value. ☀

Group economics is how we say, "Fuck waiting on the government," and change our community today. 🌙

Silence the voice in your head, the most dangerous and misleading one. Redirect your energy and attention, take control, and everything else will fall into place. ☀

GET HOME SAFE
***

Through the principles of group economics, we can preserve the ideologies and traditions of our race and culture, safeguarding them against the delusion of America's politically correct integration. 🌙

May your dreams be guided by your prayers and aligned with your purpose. The journey may be uncertain, but faith and persistence will see you through. Stay true to yourself and keep pushing forward. ☀

Instead of making assumptions, it is wiser to exercise patience and observe carefully, allowing problems or solutions to present themselves naturally. 🌙

MINDSET
***

If you lack purpose, you will seek pleasure. 🌙

Let your spirit be in the driver's seat, and your ego in the back, and watch the transformation as you become rich in the things that truly matter, like love and kindness. ☀

You're easily manipulated when you lack emotional intelligence. 🌙

GET HOME SAFE
***

Don't compare your journey with others. Your path is unique, and you should only expect what you have worked for. I don't expect a dollar more than what I worked for, but I don't want a dollar less either. ☀

Teach yourself to not react instantly off impulse because of a situation that triggered a traumatic emotion. This creates a chaotic fog in your mind and doesn't allow you the mental fortitude or emotional intelligence to recognize the trigger. Feel the internal storm, settle it so you can be at peace and come up with a solution. 🌙

I show equal respect to everyone, regardless of their background or status, as I believe respect is a free and valuable commodity. I've experienced both wealth and poverty, so I understand the importance of treating others with dignity. ☀

MINDSET
✶ ✶ ✶

We must become aware of who's gold and who's gold plated. 🌙

Live authentically, be genuine, show respect, pray sincerely, and always be grateful for the universe. Embrace who you are! ☀

Engaging in self-talk can elicit various responses from different sources within us, including the ego, the soul, the temptations of our senses, negative or positive entities, ancestors, and ultimately, God. As rational beings, it is our duty to carefully assess and evaluate these perspectives that arise from our thoughts and intuitions. However, this task is often difficult, especially when trying to differentiate between intuition and fear. It is crucial to remember that we are always in control, even when faced with confusion or uncertainty. By taking responsibility for our inner dialogue, we can develop greater self-awareness and cultivate a more profound understanding of ourselves and the world around us. 🌙

GET HOME SAFE
***

Begin each day by reflecting on five things for which to express gratitude. A daily act of thankful prayer will transform your life. ☀

Once you acquire a strong mindset, you can master any skillset. 🌙

I take pride in my roots and eagerly anticipate my destination. ☀

Rise above any circumstance. Transform yourself completely. Impermanence reigns. You are not confined. You have the power of choice. Cultivate new thoughts. Acquire new knowledge. Establish new habits. The only thing that matters is that you begin today and never look back. ☀

MINDSET
***

A disciplined and powerful mind will not allow his state of comfort to be altered by chaotic circumstances. 🌙

Honor and respect are universal languages. Let's converse. ☀

Imagination leads to manifestation. Envision yourself at your pinnacle and embody that personification. ☀

Stand firm and challenge the limits of your bravery. Be wise to not confuse bravery with stupidity. 🌙

GET HOME SAFE
* * *

I don't care how hard life gets, I'm never smoking crack, meth, or heroin. 🌙

Reprogram your mind to believe. Demonstration speaks louder than conversation. ☀

Gratitude and desire can coexist. You can be grateful and want more. 🌙

Begin each day by performing two simple tasks that can shape the trajectory of the remainder of your day: make your bed and express gratitude. ☀

MINDSET
***

Most men are being raised into a selfish ego state of consciousness where they can't comprehend being submissive to another man for a moment of time to learn from one another. I could be the biggest, strongest man in the world and not know shit about plumbing, but if a plumber comes in to teach me something, I'm going to submit my ego and take a knee for a moment so I can allow myself to fully absorb his knowledge. That doesn't make me weak. That makes me wise. 🌙

Show everyone dignity, love, and respect. Energy given out comes back in full. ☀

The mentality of being independent is really self-sabotaging humanity. We're a tribal species meant to operate as a collective village, as opposed to solely being focused on personal gain. 🌙

GET HOME SAFE
***

Each of us has a role to play and the opportunity to bring something unique and valuable to the world that only we can offer. It is our duty to contribute to a world in desperate need of our talents. Don't waste your energy on meaningless things, let's create something meaningful. ☀

Most of your day one homies are going to keep you stuck at square one. 🌙

Remember that building a strong foundation takes time, just like how diamonds need pressure to become stronger. Don't let anything bring you down. ☀

MINDSET
***

Beautiful things don't ask for attention. 🌙

My peace and worth are non-negotiable. This table is already set and situated so understand before you attempt to align yourself with my energy. ☀

You failed once and quit? Nah, you're not built for this. Failure is the pathway to success. So get the fuck up, put on a fresh pair of draws, and go back out and fail again. 🌙

I never limit myself and always think positively, imagining everything will turn out as I hope, even if it may not happen right away. ☀

GET HOME SAFE
***

Reassess how you respond to disrespect. 🌙

All my actions, thoughts, and mental state are now driven by inspiration. Unless it stems from pure love, it won't have a lasting impact. Having this perspective simplifies my tasks. My roots run deeper than just money. ☀

As quick as someone helps you out financially, is as quick as you should be to pay them back, respectfully. 🌙

MINDSET
* * *

Most people fail at business because they couldn't separate their emotions from the analytics. Sometimes it's better to be practical before you become passionate. 🌙

I used to chase perfection, but I lost sight of what's truly important in life: the message. To tap into your creative potential, you need to understand the purpose behind what you're doing. ☀

If you spend time with me, I may influence you to have faith in yourself and believe that you can achieve anything you desire in life. ☀

GET HOME SAFE
***

Imagine a raging river separating you from your life, business, or personal goals. It's natural to dream of reaching the other side, but many people fear the obstacles that lie ahead - from tree trunks and branches to anacondas and crocodiles. Yet, just like in the game Frogger, you need to plan and act on your day-to-day goals to create stepping stones towards success. One stone may take a day or two to achieve, but it can make you believe in your ability to reach your ultimate goal. The second stone may take six months, but it can help you overcome the skepticism of friends and family who don't share your vision until strangers start supporting you. The third stone may take a year to accomplish, but it can give you mental clarity, a long-term plan of action, and a healthy daily routine.

Don't be intimidated by the raging river of life. Instead, create a long-term plan of action, prepare yourself mentally, and stay resilient when faced with obstacles. Remember that success often requires patience and perseverance, and that instant gratification is not always possible. Enjoy the journey and do not fear the raging river of life. Conquer it. 🌙

MINDSET
***

Pause from reading and take action. Reach out to someone you love and let them know, or even better, go show them. In these trying times, be a source of support and help bring balance to someone's life. ☀

Don't surround yourself with five crackheads and never expect to smoke crack. 🌙

There are three types of confidence: Confidence 1 is in material possessions, and those who need these things to define themselves and assert their confidence. This can be taken away. Confidence 2 is in one's abilities, but athletes, for example, can lose it all with one injury. Confidence 3 is confidence in oneself, and these are the people who can adapt to any situation, struggle, obstacle, or setback thrown at them. This can never be taken away. ☀

GET HOME SAFE
***

This, "I ain't ever gonna change.", mentality is self-handicapping. You have to change in order to evolve. Who wants to be a Charmander forever. I want to become a fucking Charizard eventually. First, I'm going to face some obstacles in my teenage years and if I conquer and learn from them I will evolve to a Charmeleon. I'm gonna get some new moves and a new mindset. Then, I'm going to elevate from the trials and tribulations of my 20's. Acquiring more skillsets and uploading more knowledge to eventually evolve into a Charizard. Grow some wings and fly out this bitch. Embracing change is a necessary component to heightening one's consciousness. 🌙

Just hiring the best financial advisor won't necessarily help you if you don't make changes to your spending habits. You must be willing to give up unnecessary expenses and invest your money wisely to build wealth. Although I have been earning substantial income for a while, I don't let it affect my actions, decisions, or attitude. The key is to hustle, pray, plan, and invest. ☀

Forgive yourself for all the years you didn't believe in you. 🌙

MINDSET
✱✱✱

Do not allow someone else's misery to dilute your inner child. 🌙

Achieving success isn't a straightforward path. Through vocalizing your aspirations, maintaining unwavering dedication, and nurturing a constructive perspective, all other pieces will naturally align. Despite lacking a formal degree, I've engaged in discussions alongside seasoned veterinarians, scientists, and researchers boasting decades of expertise, demonstrating my competence confidently. ☀

The dating process should be treated like an interview for your future. 🌙

GET HOME SAFE
✶✶✶

The struggle between your ego and your higher purpose will be your greatest challenge. Stay true to yourself and your family will see you as legendary. ☀

In the pursuit of self-development and moral excellence, it is essential to evaluate the company we keep. One must hold their companions responsible for their actions and their effects on the group as a whole. Observe their reactions when confronted with their errors, and if they lack the capacity for self-reflection, it may be necessary to distance oneself from them. They belong on the periphery of our social sphere, not the inner sanctum of close friends and family, for they do not contribute to our growth and well-being. Who ever said only God can judge me was a fucking liar, we judge the people around us everyday. 🌙

I am not asking you to completely change yourself. I encourage you to apply the same dedication, critical thinking, and skills you use in other areas of your life, such as work, video games, or school, to your own self-improvement. ☀

MINDSET

* * *

Take a moment to reflect: are you surrounded by the same people and in the same place as ten years ago? The answer will tell you one of two things, it means either you have an amazing support system, or you are not growing. ☀

You become wise by listening and observing more than speaking. 🌙

When you free yourself from the thoughts, opinions, and influence of others, you will find peace. My mother always taught me to think for myself and be a leader, but it wasn't until I realized the power of being my own unique self that I became the best version of me. It is your birthright to be yourself, don't let anyone else's standards define you. ☀

GET HOME SAFE
***

Men who aren't in their child's life because the woman no longer wants to be with them are disrespecting their own blood line—that's not a man. 🌙

If you truly believe in yourself, your skills, and your purpose, you will also believe in those who share the same journey and remain true to their path despite challenges. Hate or envy often stem from a lack of confidence. ☀

Assess your haters. Become aware of their underlying motives. This will allow you to plan a defense or ambush them beforehand. 🌙

MINDSET
***

Killing stains the soul. 🌙

Anger clouds the mind. 🌙

Be conscious of the messages you send through your art, media, or platform. I was raised with strong values by my mother, but also aspired to be feared and respected like Mike Tyson. Remember that you may be inspiring someone, so lead by example. ☀

GET HOME SAFE
* * *

I won't allow religion, gang affiliation, ethnicity, or community to dictate whether I collaborate with someone or not. If we share common principles and goals, let's support each other. Together, we are stronger. ☀

A narrow mind is usually driven by anger. 🌙

Having followers doesn't equate to success. Success is a long journey, opinions don't matter, and the truly sincere can endure any challenge. Protect your energy and don't be swayed by what others are doing. Stay focused. ☀

MINDSET
***

It's easy to talk about gratitude and positivity, but it's more important to live it. A wise person once said, instead of debating what makes a good man, be one. ☀

If you do not conquer your mind, you will have trouble conquering your goals. 🌙

Don't be fooled by the idea that life is only about work. You have your whole future ahead of you, but don't wait to have fun. Filter out these narratives and keep pushing forward. Time doesn't wait for anyone. ☀

GET HOME SAFE
***

Don't let criticism hold you back. Not everyone will understand your message and that's okay. Focus on the people who support and believe in you, and don't let anyone discourage you for striving to be a better person. ☀

Sometimes the only way to heal a troubled mind is a listening ear. 🌙

Focus on the things that matter. It may be tempting to be impressed by material possessions or the appearance of success, but the most rewarding compliments are those that recognize the wisdom or inspiration you offer to others. The tangible items will eventually be gone, but a positive legacy will live on. ☀

MINDSET
***

Your brain is used for generating ideas, not memorizing them. Buy and use a fucking calendar for scheduling, make a fucking to-do list, and a personal filing system. Yes, we live in a bull shit matrix system, but adapt to it so you can flourish inside the belly of the beast. 🌙

It's important to stay rational and not let emotions control your actions and put yourself and your freedom in danger. Be aware of your thoughts, actions, and body language. Every situation doesn't require a reaction. Respect is a must, but also be wise and make sure you're there for your family. ☀

To change a negative cycle, check your energy. What you put out with your thoughts, actions, and words will attract the same in return. Change yourself first, and the world around you will follow. ☀

GET HOME SAFE
***

A clean room is a clean mind. 🌙

Make a to-do list and update it weekly, preferably on a day off when you clean your space and organize your life. Make a to-do list with these categories: need to do, sooner or later, and future thoughts. Better to write it down instead of trying to memorize it and eventually forgetting. Take one hour a week to be the secretary of your life. 🌙

True happiness is fulfillment, peace, and a life lived to its fullest. It is about being true to yourself, experiencing joy that does not depend on external factors. ☀

MINDSET
***

I am the shield of my family.
I protect, I provide, I produce.
I am the foundation of my family.
I guide. I mentor. I instruct.
To ensure they don't make the same mistakes I did as late in life as I did.
I will know when to rest and I will know when to push.
I bare all burdens. I bare all weathering elements: sun, rain, sleet, or snow.
I am responsible for the principles instilled in the future generations of my bloodline.
I am the head of my family. 🌙

A wise person will evolve and grow, while a fool will remain stagnant. ☀

If you want to be productive, do not put a TV in your bedroom. If you want to be really productive, do not put a TV in your house. 🌙

GET HOME SAFE
* * *

Success and fulfillment can be achieved without having to compete with others. Strive to be the best version of yourself and find your own purpose, as your unique journey was designed specifically for you. ☀

Use your phone as a tool, not a distraction.

To receive what you want in life, you must also give, including respect. ☀

MINDSET
***

Unwavering faith and tireless effort distinguish the best from the great. ☀

If one is unable to manage their thoughts and emotions, no matter their age or gender, they are still a child. 🌙

Beware of individuals who claim to have all the answers, as true mastery comes from a lifelong commitment to learning. ☀

GET HOME SAFE
***

You do not become a man because of what you're able to do physically but by what you're able to manage mentally. 🌙

Follow your heart and pursue your own vision for life, not someone else's expectations. Pursue your own greatness. ☀

Family dinner used to be regarded as a family meeting, where the family's structure was planned and organized like a company. Everyone knew their position, and discussions revolved around topics related to family ownership, including group economics, investments, health, future, and security. However, over time, this standard has deteriorated to an employee mindset, with conversations lacking long-term benefits for the family, such as gossip, entertainment, and discussions about the weather. 🌙

MINDSET
✽ ✽ ✽

To my inner perfectionist: perfection is unattainable, so evaluate, refine, and release your work. Imperfect but impactful is preferable to perfect but unseen. Improving requires consistent effort and a commitment to outdoing your previous work. ☀

Men need to learn how to take their cape off at the door, so it doesn't strangle them while they sleep. 🌙

Embrace the reflection in the mirror and watch as you transform. ☀

GET HOME SAFE
***

If your mind is scattered like a recently opened puzzle, sit and write down your thoughts. Your vision needs to be organized into position, like a finished puzzle. 🌙

Someone is looking to be inspired by your creativity and story. While it's important to share your talents, also keep in mind that you can impact and inspire others along the way. Our purpose will continue to call us until we embrace it fully. ☀

A whiteboard is an unorganized mind's best friend. 🌙

MINDSET
***

Be aware of the energy you spread into the world. Your words and actions, whether intentional or not, shape the narrative of your life. Take responsibility for the energy you bring into every interaction and make sure it aligns with the story you want to tell. ☀

Write your thoughts down. That's how you turn your ideas from fantasy to reality. 🌙

It's often our own thoughts that hold us back. Overcome self-doubt, negativity, and unrealistic expectations by being kind to yourself and remembering that everything is a work in progress, including you. Give yourself a break and be patient with your journey. ☀

GET HOME SAFE
***

Think before you speak. 🌙

Begin each day with gratitude. This ritual is not about asking for more, but about acknowledging and appreciating what you already have in your life. Focusing on what you already have instead of what you want to receive makes you more mindful and content. Express gratitude for the things that matter most, such as life, loved ones, experiences, and your family's safety. ☀

Make it a habit to become aware of your audience so you can adjust your approach before speaking to them. Your words will be rejected or absorbed based on the level of consciousness of your audience. 🌙

MINDSET
***

Distance yourself from anything or anyone that does not contribute to your personal growth. ☀

Leaving your hometown is a pre-requisite for the expansion of your intellect. Remaining within the confines of your birthplace instills a sense of complacency, inducing a cycle of unvarying habits. 🌙

Being kind doesn't cost anything and doesn't diminish one's identity. Everyone faces struggles, and the way you treat others can bring light to their battles. ☀

GET HOME SAFE

***

Avoid criticizing others' hardships, especially if you haven't experienced them yourself. Be mindful that not everyone has had the same access to resources and wisdom. Your criticism can harm both the person in pain and those who agree with you. ☀

Paying your bills is the bare minimum to this matrix. Don't expect to flourish if your standard of life is just to have your bills paid. 🌙

Judge a person by their actions towards their people, property, and principles. ☀

MINDSET
***

When pursuing long-term goals, having the right direction is more important than speed. ☀

Yin and Yang. Masculine and feminine. Ego and soul. Electricity and magnetism. Dark and light. Sun and Earth. Nature vs. technology. Silver and gold. Materialism vs. spiritualism. Independent consciousness vs. collective consciousness. Positive and negative. Artificial intelligence vs. organic intelligence. Shamans vs. doctors. Holistic vs. pharmaceutical. Opposite polarities are everywhere in the universe. Master balance. 🌙

Mindset is everything. Losers see problems and excuses, while winners see opportunities regardless of the circumstances. ☀

GET HOME SAFE
***

Inspiring others to be their best selves is just as important as striving to be your best self. ☀

Reassess how you deal with disrespect so you can become aware enough to recognize when your emotions flare up. Not every problem needs an intense response. Kings and queens evaluate issues daily and never need to raise their voice. 🌙

If you don't chase your dreams, how can you expect your children to? It's never too late to start! ☀

MINDSET
***

Faith gives us strength and the belief that we can overcome any obstacle in life. It may not always work out in the moment, but in the long term, everything happens for a reason. Keep the faith and see what unfolds. ☀

If you aim to achieve your objectives and maintain unwavering concentration, consider placing your television and gaming console in storage. 🌙

Prioritize improvement over being perfect. ☀

GET HOME SAFE
***

Stress, paranoia, worry, and resentment drain your energy. Focus on maintaining a positive mindset and high frequency. Trust the universe to handle the rest. ☀

Do you charge your phone? Don't forget to charge your body.
Do you upgrade your phone? Don't forget to upgrade your mind. 🌙

To find fulfillment, it is important to be honest with yourself and identify areas for improvement. Speak it, think it, and take action to step out of your comfort zone and grow. ☀

THANK YOU!

We are humbly honored that you took the time in reading our book on the topics of love, mindset, experience, and motivation. Your focus and enthusiasm to absorb these important guidelines for self-development is truly inspiring. In a society that prioritizes convenience and complacency, your determination to embark on a journey of self- discovery and growth through the pages of our book is what makes our work all the more meaningful.

We hope that our thoughts and experiences have served as a source of comfort, guidance, and inspiration, and that they have helped you to better understand and navigate the complexities of life. Whether you found solace in the stories of love, rewired your mind through the principles on mindset, learned from the pros and cons of our experience, or found the motivation to pursue your goals, we are honored to have imparted our insights to your consciousness and to have played a small role in your personal journey.

Once again, thank you for your time and support, we look forward to continuing to elevate and motivate you on your quest to become a better version of your previous self.

Warm regards,
Jonathan Cruz & Christopher Rodriguez

Printed in the USA
CPSIA information can be obtained
at www.ICGtesting.com
LVHW011406221223
767218LV00078B/2864